GLAD NEWS: "GOD LOVES YOU, MY MUSLIM FRIEND"

by

Samy Tanagho

Glad News: "God Loves You, My Muslim Friend"

Most of the Bible verses were quoted from New International Version © 1985 by the Zondervan Corporation with their permission included in the NIV Study Bible.

Cover and spine design by Christie Koop and Victoria Graphics, Inc., Orange, California.

Published by:
Good Shepherd World Evangelism, Inc.
3800 South Fairview Road
Santa Ana, California 92704
(714) 979-4422
e-mail: muslimministry@calvarychapel.com
www.calvarychapel.com/muslimministry

ISBN 0-9676661-9-8

PRINTED IN THE UNITED STATES OF AMERICA.

GLAD NEWS:

"GOD LOVES YOU MY

MUSLIM FRIEND"

"YOU WILL SEEK ME AND FIND ME
WHEN YOU SEEK ME WITH ALL YOUR
HEART."

JEREMIAH 29:13

CONTENTS

Prologue 1

Acknowledgments 3

Dedication 5

Introduction 7

Section One
The Testimony of the Qur'an in Regard to the
Authenticity of the Christian Scripture 11

Chapter 1
Historical Background of the Bible 13

Chapter 2
The Muslim Claim That the Bible Was Altered 21

Chapter 3
The Gospel Is God's Good News 27

Chapter 4
Did Muhammad Come to Establish a New Religion? 39

Section Two
Adam in the Qur'an and the Bible 43

Chapter 5
Adam in Islam 45

Chapter 6
The Results of the Fall 49

Chapter 7
Reconciliation Is Possible 53

Section Three
Abraham in the Qur'an and the Bible 59

Chapter 8
The Life of Abraham 61

Chapter 9
The Gospel That Was Preached to and Through Abraham 67

Section Four
Jesus in the Qur'an and the Bible 75

Chapter 10
"Christ Jesus," (Al-Masih, Isa), God's Anointed Messiah 77

Chapter 11
Jesus Christ, "His Word" (Kalimatuhuu) 89

Chapter 12
Jesus Christ, "A Spirit From God" (Ruhun Minhu) 95

Chapter 13
God Ransomed Abraham's Son 99

Section Five
Why Was Jesus Necessary? 109

Chapter 14
The Problem of Sin 111

Chapter 15
God Himself Came to Us in the Person of the Messiah 119

Chapter 16
The Incarnation of Jesus 129

Section Six
The Unique Features of Jesus 135

Chapter 17
The Virgin Birth of Jesus Christ 137

Chapter 18
The Sinlessness of Jesus Christ 141

Chapter 19
Unique Features of Jesus' Life 147

Section Seven
The Crucifixion and Resurrection of Jesus Christ 155

Chapter 20
The Crucifixion of Christ According to Islam 157

Chapter 21
The Crucifixion and Resurrection of Jesus
According to the Gospel 167

Section Eight
The Ascension and Return of Jesus Christ 177

Chapter 22
The Ascension of Jesus 179

Chapter 23
The Second Coming of Jesus 183

Section Nine
The Myth of the Three Gods of Christianity 193

Chapter 24
Do Christians Worship Three Gods? 195

Chapter 25
Understanding the Tri-Unity of God 199

Chapter 26
Jesus Is the Eternal Son of God in a Unique Spiritual Sense 207

Section Ten
What Kind of God Rules the Universe? 215

Chapter 27
Muhammad's Own Testimony 217

Chapter 28
God Is Love 221

Chapter 29
Jesus Is Unique Because He Is Our Savior 233

Bibliography 239

Notes 245

PROLOGUE

Samy Tanagho studied Islamic Law and Islamic Religion at Ain Shams University (School of Law) in Cairo, Egypt. He practiced law for many years in Egypt. He availed himself of the opportunity to study the Islamic Religion and its influence on the law and the social structure in the Arab world.

He is currently an Instructor at Calvary Chapel Bible College, Costa Mesa, California. He teaches on the topic, "How to Communicate the Good News of the Christian Scripture to the Muslim people." He has given seminars in many conferences and churches throughout the United States on this subject, and the Lord continues to provide opportunities for Samy to share his knowledge and passion.

ACKNOWLEDGMENTS

I am truly blessed by the faithfulness and submission to God of Pastor Chuck Smith. His commitment to serve our Living God and his excellent Bible teaching has inspired me. This has helped me to grow in my relationship with God during the past eighteen years. I thank him for opening his heart and Calvary Chapel to be a means of extending God's love to the precious Muslim people.

To Eileen McIlroy, you are a tireless servant of God. I appreciate all the long hours you spent to edit this book.

Thank you Marilyn Tyner, my final editor, for refining, proofing, and editing my text. God sent you my way the very last minute.

My appreciation goes to Richard and Terrie Frizzell. Richard's computer technical expertise has solved many problems. Thank you Jeff Morton for checking all the Hadith entries. And to Carl Westerlund, Director of Calvary Chapel's School of Ministry, thank you for the "read-throughs."

My appreciation to Kathleen Ciancio, Mike and Kim Kollen, for their many hours participating on this project on their computer, Jeanne Anderson, and many wonderful people at Calvary Chapel Costa Mesa for their love and prayers for the salvation of the precious Muslim people.

DEDICATION

I dedicate this book to all the precious Muslims, who are earnestly seeking to know and experience the Living God (Allah Al-Hayy).

INTRODUCTION

Everyone in this world is searching for love but for many it has proved elusive. The Beatles sang "All You Need Is Love" and then they disbanded! Many couples think they have found love but then it slips away from them, and they wonder if it was true love after all. I want to tell you about REAL LOVE, an unconditional love that will revolutionize your life. In fact, it is the greatest love story in human history —God's love for YOU!

God loves you so much, my dear Muslim friend, that He wants to embrace you as a Father embraces His child. Yes, God wants you to become His child. He wants to have a close relationship with you based on mutual love and not fear!

I personally have experienced God's deep love. In the past 23 years of my life I have met thousands of true Christians (followers of Christ) who had and still have the same experience. My desire is that many Muslims will know and experience God's deep and personal love for them. This is what has prompted me to write to you. In the Bible, 1 John 4:16, we read, "And so we know and rely on the love God has for us. God is love! Whoever lives in love lives in God, and God in him."

I want to present to you from the Qur'an and the Gospel a few important facts about the Messiah ("Isa" in the Qur'an). These undeniable facts will help you develop an informed opinion about who Jesus really is. My prayer is that you will have an open mind and a deep sincerity in your search for the truth. Also, that you will ask God before, during, and after reading this book to guide you. Finding the straight path that can lead you to know His will in your life, and what He requires of you should be the goal of us all. ("Suhuf-un-Nabien" in the Qur'an). Jeremiah 29:13 says: "You will seek Me and find Me when you seek Me with all your heart."

The first important thing I would encourage you to do is to read prayerfully the verses of the Scripture that I have mentioned in this book and allow God to show you those things He has in store for you. The Bible reveals to us that God invites us into a covenant fellowship with Himself.

Throughout its pages, the Qur'an testifies to the authenticity of the Christian Scripture, as you will discover in section one.

Samy Tanagle

SECTION ONE

THE TESTIMONY OF THE QUR'AN
IN REGARD TO THE AUTHENTICITY OF
THE CHRISTIAN SCRIPTURE

CHAPTER 1

HISTORICAL BACKGROUND
OF THE BIBLE

The Jews and the Christians are described in the Qur'an as, "the people of the Book." The Jewish Scripture is the Torah; the Christian Scripture is the Injeel. The Qur'an speaks of the Torah (Old Testament), Zabur (the Psalms), and the Injeel (Gospel) with reverence and respect. They have the status of the authentic Word of God.

Please do not believe anyone who says you should not read the Bible because it was annulled by the advent of the Qur'an. My dear Muslim friend, there is not one single verse in the Qur'an which attests that the Bible has been invalidated by the arrival of the Qur'an. Furthermore, there is no authoritative tradition (Hadith) which supports this allegation. The Qur'an itself commands Muslims to profess belief in the Bible. We read in Surah 2:136: "Say ye: 'We believe in Allah, and the revelation given to us, and to Abraham...and that given to Moses and Jesus, and that which given to (all) Prophets from their Lord: We make no difference between one and another of them: And we bow to Allah (in Islam)."

IS THE BIBLE OUTDATED?

Many Muslims mistakenly think and teach that the Qur'an came to replace the Holy Scripture of the Jews and the Christians because it became corrupted, altered, outdated, or lost. There are many Christian books which present hundreds of illustrations that give indisputable proof that the Bible is the authentic, unchanged Word of God. However, I feel compelled to briefly address the allegations that the Bible is corrupt and provide you with evidence to prove that it is not corrupt. Then you can decide what to believe.

Many years before the time of Muhammad (by A.D. 350), there was a uniform canon of the Bible. The Qur'an does not accuse Christians of changing the written words of the Holy Books of the Jews and Christians anywhere in its writing. On the contrary the Qur'an declares that it (the Qur'an) was given to confirm the previous revelations. Surah 5:48 says: "To thee [Muhammad] We sent the Scripture [Qur'an] in truth confirming the Scripture that came before it; and guarding it in safety..." This truth is repeated in many Surahs (Surah 2:8; Surah 2:101; Surah 6:92; Surah 10:37; and Surah 46:12).

The Qur'an testifies that the Torah, the Zabur, and the Injeel are the Word of God. The testimony of the Qur'an is not ambiguous. Surah 3:3–4 states: "...And He sent down the Law (of Moses) and the Gospel (of Jesus) before this as a guide to mankind..."

Regarding the Torah (the Old Testament), we read in Surah 5:44: "It was We who revealed the Law (to Moses) therein was guidance and light. By its standard have been judged the Jews, by the prophets who bowed (as in Islam) to Allah's will..." In this passage, "guidance" refers to conduct and "light" refers to spiritual insight provided by God (Allah). Other verses in the Qur'an that discuss the Torah are as follows:

Surah 2:87 reads: "We [God] gave Moses the Book and followed him up with a succession of Messengers [Jewish prophets]..."

Surah 32:23 reads: "We did indeed aforetime give the Book to Moses... and we made it a guide to the Children of Israel."

Please explore Surah 4:54; Surah 28:43; Surah 40:53-54; and Surah 45:16.

Regarding the Zabur (the Psalms), the Qur'an states in Surah 21:105: "Before this we [God] wrote in the Psalms..."

Regarding the Injeel (the Gospel), the Qur'an declares in Surah 5:46 that Christ confirmed the Torah as true and that Christ's Gospel contains guidance, light and admonition. "And in their footsteps We sent Jesus the son of Mary, confirming the law that had come before him: We sent him the Gospel: therein was guidance and light and confirmation of the law that had come before him: a guidance and an admonition to those who fear Allah." Please also read Surah 57:27.

The Qur'an confirms its support of the Torah and the Gospel and urges the Jews and the Christians to recognize the authority of their Holy Book. It says in Surah 5:68: "Say: 'O People of the Book! ye have no ground to stand upon unless ye stand fast by the Law, the Gospel, and all the revelation that has come to you from your Lord...' " Surah 5:47 states: "Let the people of the Gospel judge by what Allah hath revealed therein. If any do fail to judge by (the light of) what Allah hath revealed they are (no better than) those who rebel."

These two Surahs are a clear example to show that the Jews and Christians had the Word of God (Torah and Injeel) in their possession prior to the writing of the Qur'an. They are commanded to observe the precepts contained in them. If their Book had perished it would be impossible for them to know the commandments they must obey. If the Bible had been previously corrupted they would go astray if they obeyed it.

My dear Muslim reader, to enjoy a sincere relationship with God you must read the Gospel (the New Testament). This will increase your understanding of Isa, the Messiah (Jesus Christ). It will also help you to understand the Salvation He wants you to experience through faith in Him.

Do not believe those who tell you it is unnecessary to read the Bible. Their opinion contradicts the Qur'an itself. The Qur'an states clearly that all Muslims must follow and obey the teachings of the Torah, Zabur, and Injeel. The following Surahs are clear on this subject:

Surah 4:136 reads: "O ye who believe! Believe in Allah and His Messenger and the scripture which He hath sent to His Messenger and the scripture which He sent to those before (him). Any who denieth Allah, His angels, His Books, His Messengers and the Day of Judgment hath gone far, far astray."

Surah 2:136 states: "Say ye: 'We believe in Allah and the revelation given to us and to Abraham, Ishma'il, Isaac, Jacob and the Tribes and that given to Moses and Jesus and that given to (all) Prophets from their Lord we make no difference between one and another of them: and we bow to Allah (in Islam)."

Surah 2:285 states: "The Messenger believeth in what hath been revealed to him from his Lord, as do the men of faith. Each one (of them) believeth in Allah, His angels, His books, and His Messengers. 'We make no distinction (they say) between one and another of His Messenger.' And they say: 'We hear and we obey...' "

In Surah 2:285 and Surah 4:136 notice that "His Books" is plural. This means not just the Qur'an, but all the Holy Books. In Surah 2:136 please discern the important phrase, "We make no difference between one and another of them." This is a clear command that Muslims should regard all Holy Books as equal.

As we read in Surah 4:136 above, if the Muslim ignored or rejected any part of God's revelation in the Torah or in the Gospel he has "gone far, far astray." Also God will condemn him as an infidel as we read in Surah 40:70-72, "those who reject the Book and the (revelations) with which We sent Our messengers: But soon shall they know – when the yokes (shall be) round their necks, and the chains; They shall be dragged along — In the boiling fetid fluid; Then in the Fire shall They be burned."

The Qur'an also explains what the Jews and Christians who lived in Muhammad's time thought about the Qur'an. You can read about that in Surah 2:91: "When it is said to them: 'believe in what Allah hath sent down,' they say, 'We believe in what was sent down to us.' Yet they reject all besides, even if it be truth confirming what is with them."

Surah 10:94 is a command given to Muhammad (and to Muslims) to make the Bible the primary source of enlightenment: "If thou wert in doubt as to what We have revealed unto thee then ask those who have been reading the Book from before thee..." This verse clearly instructs all the Muslim believers to refer to the Bible when questions arise regarding the Qur'an's meaning. It is clear from this verse that in the event of any doubt about certain revelations in the Qur'an, Muhammad is commanded by God to consult with the Jews and Christians who have been reading their Holy Scriptures. Surah 10:94 is a command to Muhammad to test the truthfulness of his own message by the contents of the Holy Scriptures of the Jews and the Christians.

My dear friend, the Qur'an does not claim that God sent it (the Qur'an) to prevent corruption, alterations or disappearance of the previous Holy Books (the Torah and the Injeel). In fact, all the previous verses prove to the contrary. There are many more illustrations, such as Surah 5:43. It assures us that the Torah was available in an unadulterated form during the time of Muhammad. A dispute had arisen with the Jews in Medina; this had come to the attention of Muhammad. The Qur'an states: "But why do they come to thee for decision, when they have (their own) law before them? Therein is the (plain) command of Allah..." This verse clearly teaches that the Jews of Medina had the true Torah (Old Testament) in their possession at the time of Muhammad and it was reliable to settle their own disputes. Throughout their history, the Jews have known only the Scripture in the Books of the Old Testament, as we know them today. The Qur'an never stated that the Torah is a book different from that which the Jews themselves accept as the Torah.

The Qur'an also confirms this same fact in regard to the New Testament. The previously mentioned Surah 5:47 states: "Let the people of the Gospel judge by what Allah hath revealed therein. If any do fail to judge by (the light of) what Allah hath revealed, they are (no better than) those who rebel." How could the Christians be expected to judge by the Injeel unless they had it in their possession? The Christian world has known only one Injeel (Gospel), which existed centuries before Muhammad's time and continues to exist today. The Qur'an never stated that the Gospel was a book different from the one Christians used at the time of Muhammad. The Qur'an never accused the Jews and Christians of the world of changing the actual Biblical Manuscript.

The Qur'an in Surah 5:47 uses the word "Injeel" (Gospel), which is the same title that the followers of that Scripture used. Please refer to Mark 1:1: "The beginning of the gospel about Jesus Christ..." In fact, Christian Arabs still use the word "Injeel."

For hundreds of years after the death of Muhammad, many of the well-known early Muslim scholars upheld the integrity of the Bible. Ali Tabari's life is marked by his defense of Islam against the Jews and the Christians while he was at Baghdad (capital of the Muslim world at the time). He wrote his defense under the direction of the reigning Abbasid Caliph Mutawakkil (AD 847-861). At no time did he charge the Jews and the Christians with corrupting their scriptures. He acknowledged that the authentic Torah and Gospel remained in the hands of the Jews and the Christians. He wrote a famous book called, The Book of Religion and Empire, in which he wrote: "As to the Gospel which is in the hands of the Christians, the greater part of it is the history of the Christ, His birth and His life."

Al-Ghazali was one of the greatest Muslim theologians in the history of Islam. He never doubted the Bible's integrity. In fact, he wrote a treatise on the Trinity (about AD 1111) in which he quoted many passages from the Bible, without questioning the trustworthiness of the text. (Chapman, You Go and Do the Same, p. 53.)[1]

CHAPTER 2
THE MUSLIM CLAIM THAT THE BIBLE WAS ALTERED

This accusation that the Bible was altered raises serious questions which demand answers from those Muslims who are making the accusation. When did this alteration of the Scripture occur?

A. Before Muhammad's time?

Obviously all the verses mentioned in the previous chapter clearly show that Muhammad did not believe the Bible to be corrupt in his time.

B. After the death of Muhammad?

It is not possible that the Bible was altered after the death of Muhammad because by 600 A.D. Christianity had spread into Asia, Africa, and Europe.

It is not rational to suppose that Christians and Jews throughout the world could meet and agree on the alterations of their Holy Scripture. Historical evidence shows that major doctrinal differences have existed between Jews and Christians. They have been in disagreement regarding many religious issues.

We read in many verses in the Qur'an that Christians were divided, such as Surah 42:13-14. Surah 98:4; Surah 2:253; and Surah 3:19.

If the Scriptures were changed to alter doctrine, at least one of the many sects that existed within

Judaism and Christianity would have protested. However, there is no historical mention of such accusations or dissension. Jesus Christ never accused the Jews of altering the Scripture. On the contrary, He quoted from the Torah many times when he spoke to them. During the time of Muhammad many sincere Abyssinians scholars who were Christian (Abyssinians had befriended the Muslims) would also have exposed any attempted changes in the Scripture.

Surah 5:82 reads, "Strongest among men in enmity to the believers wilt thou find the Jews and pagans; and nearest among them in love to the believers wilt thou find those who say: 'We are Christians' because amongst these are men devoted to learning and men who have renounced the world, and they are not arrogant."

From Muhammad's time many Jews and Christians in countries conquered by the Muslim army embraced Islam. Since Muslims revere the Holy Books of the Jews and of the Christians, the Jews and Christians who became Muslims would have retained their original texts. However, no texts have been discovered that differ from today's Bible.

If the Jews and Christians had collaborated to corrupt the Bible, surely some of these converts would have been able to produce unaltered copies of the Holy Books. Hundreds of manuscripts still exist from the fourth and fifth centuries (Muhammad was born in the sixth century). These manuscripts agree with today's translations of the Scripture. Any variances were insignificant differences that did not affect any essential doctrine. Furthermore, those who had embraced

Christianity in Asia, Africa and Europe had no common language. The Bible was circulating in many different languages around the world. This makes any agreement to falsify the Holy Scripture impossible. This is especially true since these people were ignorant of any other languages.

These circumstances render it impossible for Jews and Christians to have come together after the death of Muhammad to alter their holy scriptures. We seek clarification from those people who claim that the Bible is corrupt and ask:

• When and where did this corruption take place?

• Who were the perpetrators?

• How did they reach a consensus?

• If there was an original Bible that differed, where is it so that we can compare it? And if so, specifically what textual changes were made to the original manuscripts?

HOW WAS THE BIBLE CHANGED?

Historical fact confirms that by the time of Muhammad, Judaism and Christianity were spreading throughout the world. For this obvious reason it would have been impossible for anyone to collect all the Holy Books, manuscripts and writings containing Scriptural references from all the churches, synagogues, schools, libraries and homes to make the changes. Then they would have to be returned without detection. How could they convince everyone who had a Bible to exchange it for a new, corrupted version, destroy all the original Bibles, and yet leave no evidence?

The Qur'an itself asserts that no one can alter the Word of God. "...There is none that can alter the Words (and Decrees) of Allah..." (Surah 6:34). "...No change can there be in the Words of Allah..." (Surah 6:115). Surah 10:64 and Surah 18:27 both state, "...none can change His Words..." Whoever claims that the Bible is corrupted or changed makes God a liar and accuses God of not being able to protect and preserve His Word.

Even Imam Bukhari records the following judgment of Ibn Abbas in regard to "Tahrif": The word "Tahrif" (corruption) signifies to change a thing from its original nature; and there is no man who could corrupt a single word of what proceeds from God, so that the Jews and Christians could corrupt only by misrepresenting the meanings of the words of God. (Quoted in *Hughes' Dictionary of Islam*, p. 62)

We have another very important question to ask of those who allege the Bible is corrupt. What would be the benefit?

WHAT POSSIBLE BENEFIT WOULD THERE BE FOR JEWS OR CHRISTIANS TO CORRUPT THEIR OWN SCRIPTURE?

What purpose would be served if the Christians and Jews corrupted their own Scripture? Why then would they continue to believe their Scripture? If they did this, how could they bring themselves to pass it on to their children? This is irrational and incomprehensible behavior which offers absolutely no advantage or benefit.

Some Muslims say Jews and Christians corrupted the Scripture to delete all prophecies relating to Muhammad. WHY? What would the Jews and Christians hope to gain by doing so? If such prophecies were to be found in the Bible, why would they not accept Muhammad? Also, by becoming Muslims they would have shared in the spoils given to Muslims at the conquest of Persia, Syria, Palestine, Egypt and many other countries.

Why should they bring upon themselves and their beloved children sufferings here on earth and forever by eliminating such prophecies (if any existed)? In fact, the temptation to insert prophecies of Muhammad rather than to eliminate them is more probable. By becoming Muslims they could have avoided a disadvantaged status as a minority.

CHAPTER 3
THE GOSPEL IS GOD'S GOOD NEWS

The Gospel provides the human race with clear revelation from God on how we can be saved and enjoy eternal life with God. The word "Gospel" does not refer to a book God gave to Jesus. It refers to the Glad News of God's love toward everyone. We know from reading the Gospel that Jesus Christ, a living person, is God's perfect revelation to the human race (Hebrews 1:1–4).

There is only one "Gospel" as there is only one Christ. God inspired many men through the guidance of the Holy Spirit to tell us about the person, life and teachings of Jesus. In the Bible, 2 Timothy 3:16–17 reads: "All scripture is God-breathed and is useful for teaching, rebuking, correcting and training in righteousness, so that the man of God may be thoroughly equipped for every good work." This verse means God "breathed" His Words and thoughts through His selected messengers. God is the Ultimate Author of the message and doctrines of the Gospel. Please refer to the Gospel of Luke 1:1-4 and 2 Peter 1:16-21.

Christian scholar David W. Shenk explains divine inspiration: "Divine inspiration does not mean Divine dictation." He goes on to say, "Christians do not believe that the men who wrote the Word of God were tubes through which God's words flowed. In all of the Biblical scriptures, the personality of the different writers is evident. God's inspiring activity does not cancel human involvement in the process. The Bible is the marvelous revelation in human language and thought forms. Revelation involves a profound experience of

God-man relationship, a relationship which neither compromises the sovereignty of God, nor the personhood of the man."[2]

All four Gospels—Matthew, Mark, Luke and John—are testimonies of Jesus' life and teachings. Three writers, Matthew, Mark, and John, were companions to Jesus for portions of His life.

Each writer is presenting a different aspect of the character of Jesus, the Messiah. Jesus is presented in Matthew as King. In Mark, He is presented as the servant. In Luke, written by a Greek physician, Jesus is presented as the perfect man. In the Gospel of John, written by John an eyewitness to the death and resurrection of Jesus, He is proclaimed as the Son of God. Jesus prophesied about the spreading of the Gospel seventeen times: e.g., Matthew 24:14, Matthew 26:13, Luke 21:33, and Acts 1:6-18. Jesus gave assurance that the Holy Spirit would guide their writing. See John 14:26, and John 16:13.

My dear reader, when you study the Gospel of John you are studying the Good News of the kingdom of God as taught by Jesus and authoritatively related by John a companion of Jesus. The Gospel of Luke means the Good News of Jesus Christ as recorded by Luke.

The Good News concerning Jesus is given by four writers. There is one Gospel with four presentations.

We read in the Gospel, Matthew 4:23, that, "Jesus went throughout Galilee, teaching in their synagogues, preaching the good news of the kingdom, and healing every disease and sickness among the people." The "Gospel" that our Savior and Lord Jesus Christ taught throughout His life was not fully written during His lifetime. No Muslim should view that negatively because the Hadith (Tradtions) tells us of the initial collection of the Qur'an:

> Within a year after Muhammad's death, Umar Ibn-al-khattab said to Abu Bakr, "I suggest you order that the Qur'an be collected." Abu Bakr said to him, "How can you do something which Allah's messenger did not do?" Then Abu Bakr accepted his proposal and came to Zayed and said to him, "You are a wise man and we do not have any doubts about you. So you should search for the fragments of the Qur'an and collect it." Zayed said, "By Allah, if they had ordered me to shift one of the mountains it wouldn't have been heavier for me than this ordering me to collect the Qur'an."[3]

The major method of retaining the words Muhammad uttered, which he said was given to him by the angel Gabriel, was the memory of Muhammad's companions. Portions of Muhammad's words were recorded on different materials such as palm leaves, pieces of wood, scraps of parchment and leather, tablets of stone, camel's shoulder-blades and ribs, etc.

The reason that Zayed considered the task of collecting the verses of the Qur'an so difficult was that several of Muhammad's companions (who memorized many portions of the Qur'an) had been killed in the war of the apostates, especially in the Battle of Yamama. So, how could Zayed collect the Qur'an thoroughly? Removing a mountain is much easier, as he said.

We read in one of the most reliable Islamic sources of record: "Many [of the passages] of the Qur'an that were sent down were known by those who died on the Day of Yamama... but they were not known [by those who] survived them, nor were they written down, nor had Abu Bakr, Umar or Uthman [by that time] collected the Qur'an, nor were they found with even one (person) after them."[4]

We read in one of the most authentic *Traditions*, Zayed said: "So I started looking for the Qur'an and collected it from (what was written on) palm-leaf stalks, thin white stones, and also from men who knew it by heart, until I found the last verse of Surat at-Tauba (repentance) with Abi khuzaima al-Ansari, and I did not find it with anybody other than him."[5]

Muslim scholars know very well the many extremely difficult circumstances that surrounded the first and second collection of the Qur'an. There were many controversies and disagreements among the early Muslims regarding gathering of the text, both its content and reading. These disagreements were documented in many of the well-known records of historical events by Muslim scholars and theologians.

After Abu Bakr's death, this first collection of the Qur'an was given to Umar, who entrusted it to his daughter Hafsa. The third successor to Muhammad, Uthman, commissioned Zayed and three men from Mecca to make another collection of the Qur'an. After they completed the new collection, certified copies were sent to the main provinces of the Islamic Empire. Orders were given by Uthman that all other texts must be destroyed.[6] Among these popular Qur'anic manuscripts which were destroyed is one compiled by Abdullah Ibn Mas'ud, which was the official text at Kufa, Iraq.

Muhammad instructed that Muslims should learn the Qur'an from four people. Abdullah Ibn Mas'ud is the first of the four.[7] Abdullah resented Uthman's order to burn his copy. Abdullah said that he gained possession of seventy Surahs directly from Muhammad while Zayed was still a young child.[8] Therefore, no Muslim can bring forward original manuscripts of the Qur'an written or dictated by Muhammad, since Muslims believe that it descended upon him from God through an angel. Muslims acknowledge that the Qur'an which we have today was not physically written by Muhammad.

The most important proof that the Gospel is the Word of God comes when prayerfully read. God will truly speak to you through the pages of His Word. The only reason many Muslims allege that the Bible is corrupt is that it contradicts the Qur'an in some important doctrinal areas. Needless to say, it is their responsibility to prove such allegations. The Muslims who make these claims misrepresent the Qur'an and have no evidence to prove their unfounded claims.

THE CERTAINTY OF THE BIBLE

Hundreds of books are written that present many conclusive evidences supporting the authenticity and reliability of the Bible. One of these is *Evidence that Demands a Verdict*, by Josh McDowell. This section briefly outlines some of these proofs.

People often ask, "How do we know with CER-TAINTY that any writing is from God?" The Bible commands its readers to "test everything" (1 Thessalonians 5:21). It doesn't say test everything except the Bible...it says EVERYTHING—and hold onto the TRUTH. Regardless of the opinions of friends, family or community, our own individual destiny lies in the balance. Our "choice" of a Holy Book should be carefully and prayerfully considered. God has given us minds to test such things. To ignore that gift because of pressures from others would be an affront to the One who has created us. So what kind of test is there to see if something is supernaturally inspired by God? There are three key tests:

1. Is It PROPHETIC and PROVABLE?

This is the most important test. God commanded that the test for true prophecy is that it must be fulfilled with 100% accuracy. Prophets who were not 100% accurate were deemed false and were to be stoned to death (Deuteronomy 18:20). One has to ask why such a test is in the Bible and in no other "Holy Book"? Likewise, one should ask why the Bible contains well over 600 HISTORICAL (provable) prophecies while other religious books contain almost none. Certainly, only the Holy Book of omniscient God could contain the TRUTH.

2. Is It RELIABLE?

The evidence of reliability of the Biblical manuscripts far exceeds the reliability claims of all other ancient writings. Please see the complete discussion in *Evidence that Demands a Verdict* by Josh McDowell and

The Reliability of the Bible by John Ankerberg and John Weldon.

3. Is It CONSISTENT?

The sixty-six books of the Bible were written by forty authors who came from a variety of educational and cultural backgrounds. They lived on three different continents (Africa, Asia, and Europe) and used three different languages. The Bible covers many controversial topics and was written over a period of more than 1,500 years. One would expect such a book to have significant inconsistencies in the message, symbolism, content, and most importantly the final end of the story. Who could get forty authors in a room today to agree 100% on even one controversial topic? Yet the Bible is consistent point by point throughout its text. This, itself, is a miracle.

PROPHETIC PROOF

In the Bible, in Isaiah 46:9-10, we read: "...I am God, and there is no other; I am God, and there is none like me. I make known the end from the beginning, from ancient times, what is still to come..."

To test any supposed holy work, the first consideration should be: "What proof is there?" Are words proof? Of course not, for anything can be alleged to be true. Are beliefs proof? People can be indoctrinated to believe anything. If someone can always foretell the future accurately and it is historically verifiable, it establishes that the information is from God. Think about it. If anyone or anything could accurately predict the future, except God, there would be no lottery or gambling industry today. Only God possesses the ability to KNOW what is to come. So in analyzing any purported work "from God," the first question should be: "What evidence is there that it shows divine inspiration or Prophecy?" ALL of the Bible's prophecies are historically accurate. The Bible has clear, verifiable evidence that prophecy was written in advance of the event. Only God can write history in advance!

THE BIBLE'S PROPHECIES:

The Bible contains over 600 detailed historical prophecies, which have been fulfilled. Other "holy books" may prophesy the future; only the Bible contains provable, historically verifiable ancient prophecies. These are proven to be from God and are completely supported by archaeological evidence. Some examples of fulfilled historical Old Testament prophecies are:

Prophecy of *two exiles of the Jews* (Isaiah 11:11-12 and Ezekiel 37:21).

Prophecy that *Jews would return from the Babylonian exile* in exactly seventy years (Jeremiah 25:9-11, Jeremiah 29:10-14).

Prophecy stating *the name of the Persian King, King Cyrus,* who would come hundreds of years later and authorize the rebuilding of Jerusalem (Isaiah 44:28).

Prophecy *giving the exact location the birth* of the Messiah, in Bethlehem (Micah 5:1-4).

Prophecy *foretelling the exact day when Jesus would allow himself to be called "king"* (Daniel 9:24-27)[9]

There are many other prophecies with specific details about Jesus' birth, life, ministry, trial, execution, death and resurrection. Again, every single one was fulfilled with 100% accuracy.

Another form of prophecy is the scientific information found in the Bible. This wisdom was given to Biblical authors around 2,000 years before modern science attained it. They include:

Medicine:

Principle of quarantine (Leviticus 13:45-46). Later it was used to overcome the Black Plague. Medicine: Principle of proper waste disposal (Deuteronomy 23:12-14). Today, we take it for granted.

Engineering:

The precise dimensions of Noah's Ark (Genesis 6:14-16) are deemed ideal by today's engineers.

Physics:

Second Law of Thermodynamics (Psalms 102:25-26, Isaiah 51:6, and Matthew 24:35).

Meteorology and Oceanography:

Wind and water currents (Job 36:27-28, Ecclesiastes 1:7, Isaiah 43:16 and Psalms 8:8).

Astronomy:

The earth is round (Isaiah 40:22). The earth "hangs" on nothing (in space) (Job 26:7).

Health:

The whole basis of food being clean and unclean was to provide proper sanitation and processing to avoid harmful contamination of edibles (Leviticus 7:26).

Many religious leaders have claimed their writings as holy scripture. Yet NONE can stand the test of accurate historical prophecy. Only the Bible passes the test. Its six hundred plus fulfilled historical prophecies prove without a doubt its authenticity. You will read throughout this book more about these fulfilled prophecies.

RELIABILITY

The Testimony of the Ancient Documents

Following are some facts for your consideration. Today, Christians have in their possession many ancient manuscripts of the Bible that date back many generations before Muhammad started the Islamic Religion. These manuscripts were written centuries before the Qur'an. Amazingly, our modern Bible is not significantly different from these ancient manuscripts:

1. *Codex Vaticanus* (dated 325-350 A.D.):

It includes all of the books of the Bible up to the New Testament Book of Hebrews (to Hebrews 9:14).[10] The remaining portion of the New Testament is included by a later hand. [11] Codex Vaticanus is located in the Vatican library today.

2. *Codex Alexandrinus* (dated 400 A.D.):

It contains almost the entire Bible. This original manuscript is kept in the British Museum.[12]

3. *Codex Sinaiticus* (dated 350 A.D.):
It contains the entire New Testament and a portion of the Old Testament. It is also found in the British Museum.[13]

The fact that these Manuscripts existed at least two hundred years before Muhammad even founded Islam is conclusive evidence that the only Holy Book in the hands of the Christians at Muhammad's time consisted of the same Old and New Testaments we know today.

THE OLD TESTAMENT

The Dead Sea Scrolls

The entire Old Testament, except the book of Esther, was found in 1947 in a series of caves along the northwestern portion of the Dead Sea. The documents were placed in these caves by a sect of Jews known as the Essenes, who placed parchments in clay jars and hid them in the caves near the present-day ruins of Khirbet Qumran about 70 A.D.

After scientific scrutiny, many scrolls appear to have been written at least 200 years prior to their placement in the caves in 70 A.D. The documents remained hidden, protected and forgotten for nearly 2,000 years. When reclaimed in 1947, they were compared letter by letter to today's Hebrew Bible. The scrolls showed virtually no differences.[14] This demonstrated that the Old Testament was passed down accurately. It is also apparent that the prophecies about Jesus Christ were made long before He arrived.[15]

The Septuagint

This is the Greek translation of the ancient Hebrew Holy Scriptures (now known as the Old Testament).[16] This version was transcribed sometime around 270 B.C. and is well documented in both Jewish and secular history. The content shows consistent accuracy with today's Bible. All the prophecies of the coming Messiah were translated from Hebrew into Greek almost three hundred years before Christ was born!

THE NEW TESTAMENT

The Manuscript Proliferation

Today we have nearly 24,000 early manuscripts of portions of the New Testament. This number vastly exceeds ancient works which are considered "almost perfect" today, such as Plato and Aristophanies. These original Greek New Testament manuscripts survived from as early as the first century after Christ. They form the contents of the New Testament as we have it today. And contrary to popular belief by Muslims, there is no alternative source of evidence suggesting that the life and teachings of Jesus Christ were substantially different from that which is recorded in the Bible. Not even a shred of evidence exists.

In addition to the numerous existing manuscripts (copies of first century documents), the integrity of the New Testament text is also established by applying the three basic principles of historiography. (See bibliographical test, internal test, and external test in *Evidence that Demands a Verdict*.)

CHAPTER 4

DID MUHAMMAD COME TO ESTABLISH A NEW RELIGION?

Many Muslim teachers instruct that Muhammad's mission was to establish a new religion to replace the outdated religious system of the Jews and Christians. However, according to the Qur'an itself, Muhammad's mission was not to establish a new religion but to preserve the religion of Abraham in the Torah (Old Testament).

- "So we have taught thee [Muhammad] the inspired (message), 'Follow the ways of Abraham the true in faith...' " (Surah16:123).

- "Say: 'Verily, my Lord hath guided me to a way that is straight—a religion of right—the path (trod) by Abraham the true in faith ...' " (Surah 6:161).

- "Say: 'Allah speaketh the truth: follow the religion of Abraham...' " (Surah 3:95).

- "Who can be better in religion than one who submits his whole self to Allah, does good, and follows the way of Abraham the true in faith? For Allah did take Abraham for a friend" (Surah 4:125).

THE QUR'AN ITSELF SAYS THAT MUHAMMAD DID NOT COME TO TEACH ANY NEW DOCTRINES

On the contrary, the Qur'an frequently affirms that Muhammad was given revelations to affirm what was already revealed in the Holy Books of the Jews and Christians—not to correct, replace, add to, or annul, but to confirm.

- "And before this was the Book of Moses as a guide and a mercy: and this book confirms (it) in the Arabic tongue..." (Surah 46:12).

- "Nothing is said to thee [Muhammad] that was not said to the Messengers before thee..." (Surah 41:43).

- "The same religion has He [God] established for you as that which He enjoined on Noah...and that which we enjoined on Abraham, Moses, and Jesus: namely, that ye should remain steadfast in Religion, and make no divisions therein..." (Surah 42:13).

- Say [Muhammad]: "I am no bringer of new-fangled doctrine among the messengers, nor do I know what will be done with me or with you..." (Surah 46:9).

SECTION TWO

ADAM IN THE QUR'AN AND THE BIBLE

CHAPTER 5
ADAM IN ISLAM

The Qur'an, in Surah 2:30, states that Adam was God's representative (Khalifah). Abdullah Yusuf Ali commented on this verse in *The Meaning of the Holy Qur'an*, (footnote 47). He said that the power of will when used aright brings the man nearer to the God-like nature. We read in Surah 15:29, "When I have fashioned him and breathed into him of My Spirit..." In Surah 2:34 we read: "...Behold we said to the angels. Bow down to Adam and they bowed down..." Al-Ghazzali wrote that God created Adam in His own form (see *Shorter Encyclopedia of Islam*, p.40). Adam and Eve were able to enjoy a perfect communion with God. God gave them perfect circumstances. He gave them everything they needed.

We know from the Bible and the Qur'an that Satan tempted and deceived Adam and Eve and they failed to represent God. By trying to become independent they disobeyed and sinned. We clearly see that in Surah 2:36: "Then did Satan make them slip from the (Garden) and get them out of the state (of felicity) in which they had been. We said: 'Get ye down, all (ye people), with enmity between yourselves. On earth will be your dwelling place and your means of livelihood for a time."

The Qur'an is in agreement with the Bible in reference to the fall of Adam and Eve. They ate of the forbidden fruit. Also in Surah 2:36, the form used is the imperative "fall down" (in Arabic ahbituu), which means "get down, descend, crash down."[17] The widely acclaimed Muslim scholar and commentator of the Qur'an, Pickthall, says: "Here the command is in the plural, as addressed to Adam's race."[18]

Abdullah Yusuf Ali, commented on Surah 2:36, "Get ye down ye people" in his widely recognized translation and commentary of the Qur'an: "Allah's decree is the result of man's action. Note the transition in Arabic from the singular number in Surah 2:33 to the dual in Surah 2:35 and the plural here, which I have indicated in English, 'All ye people.' Evidently Adam is the type of all mankind..."[19]

This clearly means that God cast Adam and Eve and all those who were to be born to them, future generations, out of Paradise. This penalty was for the disobedience of Adam and Eve as parents. Everyone that has descended from Adam and Eve has been punished. The Qur'an clearly teaches the fall of Adam and also implicates the whole human race in this fall. In Surah 2:38 we read the same command was given to Adam and Eve with all their offspring, "Get ye down all [jami] from here." Surah 2:36 and Surah 7:22-24 of the Qur'an state plainly that Satan deceived Adam and Eve and caused their fall. The Qur'an says that they were created in heaven itself and enjoyed peace and felicity until they disobeyed God and were cast out of heaven. God (Allah) cast them down to earth with enmity between each other.

Note the word used in Surah 2:38, "Get ye down all [jami] from here." The Arabic word "jami" as used in this verse is taken to mean a "host, congregation, all, together, altogether."[20] Therefore, it is obvious that the order to depart from the Garden was intended to cover all mankind. An authentic well-known Hadith[21] confirms this truth: "The prophet Moses in disputing and taking exception to Adam saying, 'O Adam, you are our father yet you failed us, that is, you made us fall in disappointment which is deprivation (and brought us out of paradise) that is, you were the cause of our expulsion from the place of bliss and permanence, to the place of misery and ruin.'"[22]

There is more documentation in the Qur'an and Hadith that refers to the responsibility of Adam as the representative of the human race. However, the evidence previously supplied is adequate. Adam is the first human created. We all originate from him. It is from this point of origin that mankind has had to face its ultimate problem: the results of Adam's fall into sin.

CHAPTER 6
THE RESULTS OF THE FALL

According to the Gospel, "When God created man, His purpose was that man might enjoy constant and beautiful fellowship with Him. So God placed man in the Garden of Eden. The Bible speaks about God coming into the garden and communing with man. God's intent for man was fulfilled as Adam walked in fellowship with God. But we read that Adam disobeyed and that sin entered the human race. Adam's fellowship with God was broken as a result of sin. This is always the effect of sin. For the prophet Isaiah tells us that God's hand is not short that He cannot save, neither is His ear heavy that He cannot hear. But your sins have separated you from your God (Isaiah 59:1-2)."[23]

No one can make light of Adam's sin by saying that he just forgot God's command. Adam could not possibly forget the only command God gave him, which the devil reminded him of (Surah 7:20). Adam was granted the freedom to choose. The moment Adam and Eve ate of the forbidden tree, they intentionally challenged and violated the authority of God. Their sin was an act of defiance against the Almighty God.

The sin of Adam and Eve had a devastating effect on the whole human race. The effect of their sin became universal and the whole human race was sent to a world where sin and death reign.

The Hadith (Tradtions) is the recorded sayings, advice, and actions of Muhammad, the prophet of Islam. The majority of the Muslim scholars of the world believe that the collections of the Hadith, in *Al-Bukhari and Muslim*, are regarded as Holy Books in addition to the Qur'an. They are inspired by Allah. In the Hadith we read that Muhammad said: "Every son of Adam is a sinner."[24] In a famous Hadith, Muhammad said: "None is killed unjustly, but the first son of Adam will have a part of its burden... a part of its blood because he was the first to establish the Tradtions of murdering."[25] Muhammad said in a well-known reliable Tradtions, "Whenever a person is murdered unjustly, there is a share from the burden of the crime on the first son of Adam for he was the first to start the Tradtions of murdering."[26] My dear friend, sin became an integral part of the human nature as an immediate result of Adam's sin and disobedience. For this reason, the Qur'an states in Surah 2:36: "With enmity between yourselves" or paraphrased "all of you will become hostile to each other."

God created man in His own image. He gave him freedom of choice, and man chose to rebel against God in the person of Adam. Sin distorted God's image in man. The human nature fell captive to the power of sin. It became intrinsically corrupt and unable to purify itself completely as it was before the Fall. Muhammad, the prophet of Islam, said, "Satan runs in the body of Adam's son, i.e., man, as his blood circulates in it..." [27] Muhammad also said, "Satan circulates in the human mind as blood circulates in it..." [28]

According to the Qur'an, Adam repented. God accepted his repentance but that alone did not reverse the effect of sin. It permanently and indelibly tainted the human nature. Because of sin neither Adam nor his descendants were able to remain in the Garden where God had placed them. They were never allowed to go back. Adam's repentance did not stop the effect of sin. The human race experiences it daily through jealousy, envy, hate, etc. None of Adam's descendants are able to live the pure and sinless life which God created man to live. All humans are captive to the power of sin, as indicated in the following:

- Surah 12:53: "...the (human) soul is certainly prone to evil..." All of us can testify that we are prone to satisfy the lust of the flesh. All of us violate our conscience and have the tendency to yield to our selfish nature habitually.

- Surah 16:61: "If Allah were to punish men for their wrongdoing, He would not leave, on the (earth), a single living creature..."

The human being that God created was perfect. The Fall affected each part of our nature. Our body dies a physical death. Our soul dies a mortal death. Our spirit dies a spiritual death. Communication with God was broken when the first sin was committed.

Alienation from God is the first result of that spiritual death which came to us as the result of sin. Romans 5:12 states, "Therefore, just as sin entered the world through one man, and death through sin, and in this way death came to all men, because all sinned." A Christian scholar calls it, "The most dreadful of all sin's consequences." All men sin because sin is an integral part of the human nature. Sinfulness pervades mankind individually and collectively.

It is apparent that the circumstances of life did not bring sin to man, it is man who brought sin to the world. It is clear that the descendants of Adam inherited all the characteristics of his fallen nature. As a consequence they became subject to the condemnation of God because people's sins are committed against the Holy and Righteous God who cannot tolerate sin. So we read in the Gospel, Romans 6:23: "The wages [consequences] of sin is death." This is God's law and justice.

CHAPTER 7
RECONCILIATION IS POSSIBLE

The Gospel declares, "For since death came through a man, the resurrection of the dead comes also through a man. For as in Adam all die, so in Christ all will be made alive" (1 Corinthians 15:21-22). The Good News that God wants you to know is, "God is love" (1 John 4:16). His nature is love. You will surely discover this glorious fact by the time you finish reading this book. Therefore, He planned a way to save mankind. God's holiness demanded justice that punishes the sinners while His love pleaded for mercy and forgiveness. The Living Word of God, Jesus Christ, became flesh, and on the cross He suffered the consequences of our sin. God's judgment fell upon Jesus. On our behalf, Christ voluntarily paid the price that we should have paid for all the sins that we have committed and will commit against God.

The Gospel in Luke 4 teaches that Satan (Shaitan) tempted Jesus to become independent from God's will and to accept the kingdoms of the world from Satan. Unlike Adam and Eve, Jesus had complete victory over Satan's temptations. In the Gospel, Jesus is recognized as the perfect man who submitted totally every minute of His life to the will of God.

All of the prophets and people throughout human history have yielded to Satan's temptations and sinned frequently. Jesus was the only exception. By the admission of the Qur'an and the Gospel, He was the only man to live a life without committing one single sin. In the Gospel, the book of Romans states:

"But the gift is not like the trespass. For if the many died by the trespass of the one man, how much more did God's grace and the gift that came by the grace of the one man, Jesus Christ, overflow to the many! Again, the gift of God is not like the result of the one man's sin: The judgment followed one sin and brought condemnation, but the gift followed many trespasses and brought justification. For if, by the trespass of the one man, death reigned through that one man, how much more will those who receive God's abundant provision of grace and of the gift of righteousness reign in life through the one man, Jesus Christ. Consequently, just as the result of one trespass was condemnation for all men, so also the result of one act of righteousness was justification that brings life for all men. For just as through the disobedience of the one man the many were made sinners, so also through the obedience of the one man the many will be made righteous" (Romans 5:15-19).

The Bible speaks about "creation," which is generation, and then degeneration and regeneration. Teaching about regeneration, Jesus declared, "I tell you the truth, no one can see the kingdom of God unless he is born again" (John 3:3). Because of our sin, we are spiritually dead and kept out of the holy presence of God. However, if you believe in what Jesus Christ (AL-Masih Isa) did for us on the cross, and you confess your sins and repent, you will be born again! You will be allowed into the presence of God. That means you will begin to enjoy a peaceful, personal, and living relationship with your Creator!

What does it mean if you become a born-again Christian?
You will be a new creature in your heart and trans-
formed from the very depths of your being. God will
give you a new heart, new affections and desires, new
power and new purpose, new view of people around
you, a new nature, and a new destination! The Bible
declares, "If anyone is in Christ, He is a new creation..." (2 Corinthians 5:17). Adam was the head of
the old creation and Christ is the head of the new creation.

Who is truly a Christian? All true believers and followers of Christ experience a new birth. Note that
there are many people who claim to be Christians
because they either had Christian parents, or a
Christian education, or because they were born in
America, or believe that Christianity is a good religion.
Or, they might be attending a church, or trying to do
good works, or agreeing with Christianity merely intel-
lectually. However, none of those things can make anyone a true Christian or child of God. Only those people
who experience the new birth, as explained in the
above paragraph, are truly Christians. The evidence of
the new birth is the presence of the Holy Spirit within,
confirming that someone is a child of God. We read in
the Bible, in Ephesians 2:1-5:

> "As for you, you were dead in your
> transgressions and sins, in which you
> used to live when you followed the ways
> of this world and of the ruler of the
> kingdom of the air, the spirit who is now
> at work in those who are disobedient.
> All of us also lived among them at one

time, gratifying the cravings of our sinful nature and following its desires and
thoughts. Like the rest, we were by
nature objects of wrath. But because of
His great love for us, God, who is rich in
mercy, made us alive with Christ even
when we were dead in transgressions."

God showed us His mercy through Jesus Christ.
Even the Qur'an states that Jesus is a mercy from
God. "...And (we wish) to appoint him...a Mercy from
us..." (Surah 19:21).

Because of Jesus, we can trade judgment for forgiveness. We can trade our sin for the righteousness of
Jesus. Christ offers us the opportunity to be born into
His spiritual family. Jesus is alive now. He alone can
give us eternal life in the presence of God. Jesus came
to us and was given by God to bring us into fellowship
with God by taking away our sins through dying in our
place.

The Bible states, "All this is from God, who reconciled us to himself through Christ... not counting
men's sins against them..." (2 Corinthians 5:18-19).

SECTION THREE

ABRAHAM IN THE QUR'AN AND THE BIBLE

CHAPTER 8

THE LIFE OF ABRAHAM

Abraham was given the title "friend of God" in both the Qur'an and the Bible. Surah 4:125 teaches, "...For Allah did take Abraham for a friend." In the Gospel, in James 2:23 we find that Abraham is described as the "friend of God." The title suggests a very close relationship to God. It implies that God shared with Abraham many of His secret plans for the future that He would not otherwise reveal to someone who was only His servant.

Abraham is the "father of all true believers." The Qur'an in Surah 3:95 also exhorts Muslims, "...follow the religion of Abraham, the sane in faith..." In the Bible, Galatians 3:7, we read, "Understand, then, that those who believe are children of Abraham."

Abraham was "an example of the true religion" to come and a model for Muslims. Please read Surah 2:130. Abraham is also a model for all true Christians. All true believers in the Gospel have saving faith as Abraham had (Galatians 3:8, 9). Abraham was a prototype of the true religion to come.

ABRAHAM'S SON — ISAAC OR ISHMA'IL?

Abraham received a promise from God that He would give him a son. Abraham was fully aware of the physical impossibility for his wife Sarah to have a son. She was barren. Abraham believed that God would fulfill His promise supernaturally. The Bible teaches that this promised son was Isaac. Please read Genesis 17:15-21.

AL-Tabari, the prominent Muslim Arab historian, filled several pages of his first volume with *Traditions* (Hadith), indicating that Isaac was to be sacrificed. There are three more pages with famous traditions that clearly say it was Ishma'il.[29] It is a fact that the Hadith supports both points of view equally. Indeed the majority of the early traditions state that it was Isaac. AL-Thalibi expressly states that the Ashab, Companions of the Prophet, and the Tabuin, Successors of the Companions, from Umar Ibn AL-Khattab to Kab AL-Ahbar, believed that the person to be sacrificed was Isaac.[30]

The Qur'an confirms that the only son promised to Abraham by God was Isaac. God commanded Abraham to sacrifice his son. The only reference that relates to the sacrifice of the son of Abraham is Surah 37:99-107: "...so we gave him the good news of a boy ready to suffer and forbear... 'O my son! I see in vision that I offer thee in sacrifice...'" This passage does not say which son it was, however, this passage does indicate that it is the same son whose birth was described as "Good News."

Just two verses after the mention of the sacrifice, Isaac is mentioned in Surah 37:109-113: "Peace and salutation to Abraham... and we gave him the good news of Isaac... we blessed him and Isaac..." Earlier in the Qur'an, in Surah 29:27, we read, "And We gave (to Abraham) Isaac and Jacob and ordained among his progeny Prophethood and Revelation..." Isaac's birth is also foretold as good news in Surah 11:71: "...But we gave her Glad tidings of Isaac..."

We read again about Isaac and his mother Sarah in Surah 51:28-30, "...and they gave him Glad tidings of a son..."; "...his wife came forward (laughing) aloud! She smote her forehead and said, 'A barren old woman...'"

The Qur'an has no reference to the birth of Ishma'il. It never foretold that Abraham would be the father of Ishma'il. Nowhere in the Qur'an was it ever specifically stated that Ishma'il was promised to Abraham by name as Isaac was. Very little is said in the Qur'an about Ishma'il, and absolutely no attention is given to his mother or his sons. It is apparent that the son about whom the good news was given and the one to be sacrificed as mentioned in Surah 37:99-107 was not Ishma'il but Isaac.

Many objective and educated Muslims acknowledge that the evidence points to Isaac as the promised son. For this reason Abdullah Yusuf Ali, in his internationally acknowledged commentary of the Holy Qur'an, made a significant admission, "The boy thus born was according to Muslim Tradtions (which, however, is not unanimous on this point), the first born son of Abraham, VIZ., Ishma'il."[31]

Please note the wording: "According to Muslim Tradtions" and "which, however, is not unanimous." We see clearly that the claim that the son was Ishma'il is not according to the Qur'an. The evidence from the Qur'an is conclusive that Ishma'il is not the son announced of God. In fact, one of the most famous and explicit narratives in the Jewish and Christian Scripture, is God's command to Abraham to sacrifice Isaac (James 2:21). If Muhammad believed that what is recorded in the Jewish and Christian Scripture is not correct, he certainly would have declared in the Qur'an that the son to be sacrificed was Ishma'il and not Isaac.

THE TEST AND ABRAHAM'S FAITH

"Some time later God tested Abraham. He said to him, 'Abraham!' 'Here I am,' he replied. Then God said, 'Take your son, your only son, Isaac, whom you love, and go to the region of Moriah. Sacrifice him there as a burnt offering on one of the mountains I will tell you about' " (Genesis 22:1-2). Abraham thought deeply about God's shocking and unusual command. We know from Scripture God promised Abraham that through his son, Isaac, he would have many descendants, "...as numerous as the stars in the sky and as countless as the sand on the seashore" (Hebrews 11:12).

Genesis 21:12 attests, "...it is through Isaac that your offspring will be reckoned." Abraham believed God to be ever faithful. Therefore, God's promise that he would have many descendants through Isaac would be fulfilled. How could Abraham have the descendants promised to him if he sacrificed his son Isaac as God had commanded? Abraham believed the promises of God, His faithfulness and righteousness. Hence, he concluded that the only way Isaac could beget offspring, if he was to be sacrificed, would be if God brought him back from the dead. The Qur'an in Surah 2:260 states, "Behold! Abraham said: 'My Lord! Show me how Thou givest life to the dead...' " Abraham reasoned that if God could give him a son when it was naturally impossible to have one, then God could also raise him back to life from the dead.

The Bible makes it very clear that this was Abraham's conclusion: "By faith Abraham, when God tested him, offered Isaac as a sacrifice. He who had received the promises was about to sacrifice his one and only son, even though God had said to him, 'It is through Isaac that your offspring will be reckoned.' Abraham reasoned that God could raise the dead, and figuratively speaking, he did receive Isaac back from death" (Hebrews 11:17-19).

CHAPTER 9
THE GOSPEL THAT WAS PREACHED TO AND THROUGH ABRAHAM

In Romans 4:17, we read that God told Abraham, "'...I have made you a father of many nations...'" Abraham reasoned why should he be made a leader for mankind and the father of the faithful. So Abraham saw his chosen status as a reflection of God's great glory in heaven. He realized that he was merely a type of the true heavenly Father.

If he was only a type, then Isaac's unique miraculous birth, the sacrifice, the resurrection from the dead, and the innumerable descendants were also all types of a greater reality yet to come. Abraham realized that the Risen Son would be the source of the great blessings to the world.

ABRAHAM PUTS IT ALL TOGETHER
The Father would have a Son born in this world in unusual circumstances through the intervention of the Holy Spirit. The Son was to be offered as a sacrifice to God by the hand of His own Father. He would rise from the dead and the risen Son would be the source of blessings to the world. God revealed to his friend Abraham His plan of salvation and the blessing to mankind. Abraham foresaw the heart of the Gospel. Jesus told the Jews, "Your father Abraham rejoiced at the thought of seeing my day; he saw it and was glad" (John 8:56).

We read in Genesis 22:7-8 that Isaac spoke up and said to his father Abraham, "The fire and wood are here... but where is the lamb for the burnt offering?" Abraham did not know that a lamb was going to be substituted. Abraham truly believed that he would sacrifice his son. Abraham said to Isaac, "God Himself will provide the lamb for the burnt offering, my son." The original words in Hebrew are: "God gives of Himself the Lamb for the offering." Obviously Abraham had another lamb in mind. In other words, Abraham's answer to Isaac was in essence, "My son, I must offer you as a sacrificial lamb to God. I want you to know that God will give of Himself a lamb as a sacrifice. The Heavenly Father will sacrifice His own son as a lamb for the salvation of the world." Through this experience God revealed to Abraham and to us that He would send His own Son to die for the sins of the world. After centuries of sacrificing animals in the Temple, John the Baptist proclaimed and testified about Jesus. You can read his words in John 1:29: "The next day John saw Jesus coming toward him and said, 'Look, the Lamb of God, who takes away the sin of the world!' "

How awesome it is to realize that 2,000 years after God asked Abraham to sacrifice his son Isaac on Mt. Moriah, Jesus was crucified on that same Mt. Moriah. Genesis 22 is a foreshadow of the crucifixion of Jesus Christ according to God's plan of redemption for mankind. *The righteousness of Abraham resulted not from his works but from his faith.* The Bible states that the true children of Abraham were those who had his faith, regardless of race or ancestry. Consider Abraham: He believed God, and it was credited to him as righteousness. Understand, then, that those who believe are the children of Abraham. The Scripture foresaw that God would justify the Gentiles by faith, and announced the Gospel in advance to Abraham: "All nations will be blessed through you." So those who have faith are blessed along with Abraham, the man of faith (Galatians 3:6-9).

In spite of Abraham's sins, which are recorded in the Bible and the Qur'an (Surah 26:82), God forgave him and declared him to be righteous. Abraham's faith in God's ability to perform what He promised was accepted by God as righteousness. Abraham depended on the righteousness, goodness, and trustworthiness of God. Thus his faith glorified God. As Abraham was saved by faith (Genesis 15:6, Romans 4:2-5), the real children of Abraham are those who have faith rather than those who rely on their ability to keep all the laws of God. Everyone who has faith receives the blessing of justification. Abraham's righteous status before God did not come from his own piety but came as a result of his faith in God's grace and faithfulness. Please read Romans 4:20-25:

> "Yet he did not waver through unbelief regarding the promise of God, but was strengthened in his faith and gave glory to God, being fully persuaded that God had power to do what he had promised." This is why it was credited to him as righteousness. The words, it was credited to him were written not for him alone, but also for us, to whom God will credit righteousness — "for us who

believe in him who raised Jesus our
Lord from the dead. He was delivered
over to death for our sins and was
raised to life for our justification."

In Galatians 3:14, we read: "He redeemed us in
order that the blessing given to Abraham might come
to the Gentiles through Christ Jesus, so that by faith
we might receive the promise of the Holy Spirit."

Abraham looked ahead to the coming of his greater
son, Jesus, whom he knew would be the Son of God.
For this reason Jesus is called the son of Abraham
(Matthew 1:1). We read that God promised Abraham,
"through your offspring all nations on earth will be
blessed..." (Genesis 22:18).

The Apostle Paul explained in his letter to the
church in Galatia the meaning of these words, which is
the promise God made to Abraham, "The promises
were spoken to Abraham and to his seed. The
Scripture does not say, 'and to seeds,' meaning many
people, but 'and to your seed,' meaning one person,
who is Christ" (Galatians 3:16).

The Bible clearly tells us that Jesus, the Messiah,
who descended from Abraham, came to accomplish our
salvation. Jesus' coming fulfilled God's promise to
Abraham of the blessings of all people. Through believing in Him, people from all nations receive the blessings of God.

Have you ever wondered, my friend, why God chose
to ask Abraham to give his son rather than his sheep,
land or houses? It is because a man's own son is more
precious to his heart than anything else. If Abraham is

willing to give his own son to God, then he is prepared to give God anything and everything. Therefore, the best way for God to test Abraham's love for Him was to command him to sacrifice his son.

Abraham confirmed his great love for God when he was willing to give Him his son as a sacrifice. And God confirmed His sacrificial love for us in this same way. This is exactly what God wants you to discover, my dear Muslim friend. He expressed His perfect love for you. "He who did not spare his own Son, but gave him up for us all—how will he not also, along with him, graciously give us all things?" (Romans 8:32). Here we see God's heart aflame with love for mankind.

God would never ask any man to do more for Him than He was willing to do for man. Abraham knew that what God commanded him to do was no more than what God was willing to do for him. Please allow me to ask you a question: Do you think God would ask a greater expression of love from man than God would give to man? Would he require a deeper demonstration of love from us than what He would demonstrate for us? If you said yes, then we must conclude that Abraham gave a greater proof of his deep love for God than God has ever given for mankind in return. Do you feel comfortable believing that? The Gospel tells us in Romans 5:8, "But God demonstrates his own love for us in this: while we were still sinners, Christ died for us." Jesus Himself said in the Gospel of John, "Greater love has no one than this, that he lay down his life for his friends" (John 15:13). God bestowed on us the greatest form of love. That love is stronger than death and cannot be defeated by it. The true followers of Jesus know for sure that God is willing to give us His best and will not withhold anything good from us.

Further, God's love for us can be demonstrated by comparing two military leaders. One leader orders his troops into battle while he stays out of the fight watching from a safe place as his men give their lives in battle. The other leader orders his troops into battle, but he joins them on the front lines leading them to victory. He is willing to lay down his life for his men and their cause. This is how God has led His people to victory, even giving of Himself for their sake.

SECTION FOUR

JESUS IN THE QUR'AN AND THE BIBLE

CHAPTER 10
"Christ Jesus," (Al-Masih, Isa), God's Anointed Messiah

In Surah 4:171, the Qur'an gives Jesus three distinguished titles: "...Christ Jesus (Al-Masih, Isa), the son of Mary, ...and His Word, (Kalimatuhuu)... and a Spirit proceeding from Him: (Ruhun Minhu)..."

Jesus alone is referred to as AL-Masih, "The Messiah," in the Qur'an. The definite article ("the") positively distinguishes Jesus from all the other prophets. Occasionally, He is referred to solely by this title without being referred to by name, as in Surah 4:172. Jesus is given the title Messiah more than ten times in the Qur'an. For example in Surah 3:45, we read the angel Gabriel first appeared to Mary and stated that the name of her son was to be "...the Christ Jesus..." (AL-Masih Isa).

Jesus is called the Messiah in the Hadith. The Qur'an does not explain the meaning of this title. Many respected Muslim scholars such as Al Zamakshari and AL-Baidawi have admitted that the word "Messiah" was not an original Arabic word. AL-Baidawi, commenting on Surah 3:45, says that the word "Christ" (AL-Masih) was originally a Hebrew word (Mashih). Thus, the Qur'an by not giving an explanation of this title, is implicitly accepting what is written about the Messiah in the Christian Scripture.

It is important to note here that the Gospel was written in the Greek language. The Greek word for AL-Masih or "The Anointed One" was "ho Christos," from which comes the English word "Christ." Therefore, whenever you see the word "Christ" in the English translation of the New Testament, it means the same as AL-Masih. All the Muslim scholars agree on this point.

Prophecy of the Coming Messiah

The Old Testament (the ancient Hebrew Holy Scriptures) was written between 400 and 2,000 years before Christ came to earth. It contains many prophecies of One Glorious Savior, who according to God's Word, would one day be sent by God. He is called "the Messiah." Incredibly, the Old Testament contains over 300 references to the coming Messiah, which were fulfilled in the life of Jesus. It cannot be said that the "fulfilled prophecies" regarding Jesus were fabricated because many of the prophecies concerning the Messiah were totally beyond the human control of Jesus. Notice the following examples:

Place of Birth:

He was born in Bethlehem, which was foretold by Micah about 700 years before the coming of Christ (Micah 5:2). The account of the fulfillment of this prophecy is found in Matthew 2:1,6 and John 7:42.

The Manner of His Birth:

He was born of a virgin. "Therefore the Lord himself will give you a sign: The virgin will be with child and will give birth to a son, and will call him Immanuel" (Isaiah 7:14). We see the fulfillment of this prophecy in Matthew 1:18-25, and Luke 1:26-35.

His Death by Crucifixion:

It was foretold by David 1,000 years before the coming of Christ, "...they have pierced my hands and my feet" (Psalms 22:16). It is particularly significant that this was written about 600 years before crucifixion was used for execution.

The details of His death and burial were given by Isaiah about 700 B.C. Isaiah 53 not only tells us what is going to happen to the Messiah, but also tells us why: "But he was pierced for our transgressions, he was crushed for our iniquities; the punishment that brought us peace was upon him, and by his wounds we are healed. We all, like sheep, have gone astray, each of us has turned to his own way; and the LORD has laid on him the iniquity of us all" (Isaiah 53:5-6).

THE QUR'AN CONFIRMS THAT GOD REVEALED THE PSALMS TO DAVID

My dear Muslim friends, the Qur'an informs us in Surah 2:136: "Say ye, 'We believe in Allah, and the revelation given to us, and to Abraham, Ishma'il, Isaac, Jacob, and the Tribes and that given to Moses and Jesus, and that given to (all) Prophets from their Lord: We make no difference between one and another of them...' " The prophets referred to in Surah 2:136 include David. Surah 4:163 informs us, "...and to David We gave the Psalms." (Also refer to Surah 17:55.) Surah 21:105 states: "Before this we [God] wrote in the Psalms..."

CHRIST IN THE PSALMS

Both the Jewish and Christian faiths have long believed that many Psalms referred as much to the promised Messiah as they did to events at the time. Many of the passages in Psalms describe in detail events from Christ's life and death. Yet they were written hundreds of years before Christ (B.C.). (See Table 1.)

Reference in Psalms	Reference to Christ	Fulfillment in the New Testament
Psalm 2:7	The Messiah will be the Son of God	Matthew 3:17; Matthew 16:16; Luke 9:35; Luke 22:70; John 1:34,49
Psalm 68:19	He ascended into heaven.	Ephesians 4:8-10
Psalms 96:13	He will return to judge the world.	1 Thessalonians 1:10; John 5:22,23
Psalm 110:1	He is David's son and David's Lord. He shall be called Lord.	Matthew 22:41-45 (Jesus recited the words of Psalm 110:1 and applied them to Himself.)
Psalm 16:9-11	The Resurrection.	Acts 2:22-32
Psalm 2:1-12	The true nature of Christ.	Acts 4:24-28
Psalm 69:21	Jesus was thirsty.	John 19:28-30 (Jesus' words on the cross.)
Psalm 22:16	He would be crucified.	Matthew 27:35
Psalm 41:9	He would be betrayed by a friend.	Matthew 26:47-50

Table 1

CHRIST IN THE BOOKS OF THE PROPHETS

In Luke 24:44, Jesus said to his disciples, "This is what I told you while I was still with you: Everything must be fulfilled that is written about me in the Law of Moses, the Prophets and the Psalms." We read another wonderful prophecy in Isaiah 9:6, "For to us a child is born, to us a son is given, and the government will be on his shoulders. And he will be called Wonderful Counselor, Mighty God, Everlasting Father, Prince of Peace."

The coming Messiah will be called "Immanuel." Immanuel is a Hebrew name meaning "God with us." We read this prophecy in Isaiah 7:14, "Therefore the Lord himself will give you a sign: The virgin will be with child and will give birth to a son, and will call him Immanuel." We see the fulfillment of this prophecy in Matthew 1:23, "The virgin will be with child and will give birth to a son, and they will call him 'Immanuel' — which means, 'God with us.' " We read another prophecy in Isaiah 50:6 that the Messiah was spat on and struck: "I offered my back to those who beat me, my cheeks to those who pulled out my beard; I did not hide my face from mocking and spitting." This was fulfilled in Matthew 26:67, "Then they spit in his face and struck him with their fists. Others slapped him."

We read in Daniel 7:13-14: "In my vision at night I looked, and there before me was one like a son of man, coming with the clouds of heaven. He approached the Ancient of Days and was led into his presence. He was given authority, glory and sovereign power; all peoples, nations and men of every language worshiped him. His dominion is an everlasting dominion that will not pass away, and his kingdom is one that will never be destroyed." Again, there are a total of 330 prophecies in the Old Testament about Jesus, and all were fulfilled with 100% accuracy! Many books have been written on this subject.

Jesus called Himself "the Son of God" as in the Gospel, Matthew 26:63-64. Jesus also called Himself "the Son of Man" to make His claim to humanity evident, but specifically because:

- In the Syriac language, which was His mother-tongue, the expression "Son of Man" is continually used to denote man.

- The promise that a man, one of Adam's descendants, the seed of the woman, would crush the serpent's head (Genesis 3:15). Christ was the person to whom this referred.

- Daniel 7:13 uses the title to denote the Coming Messiah, who is Jesus.

Most of the Jews thought they were special and superior to all other races of peoples. The Jewish men thought they were better than slaves and women. They were incorrect. God declared in His word that all believers are one in Christ. Having faith in Christ transcends people's differences. Galatians 3:28 reads: "There is neither Jew nor Greek, slave nor free, male nor female, for you are all one in Christ Jesus."

The Jewish leaders were mistaken when they expected the Messiah to elevate their nation. They were also mistaken when they believed Messiah would establish Himself as an earthly king. Jesus declared,

"My kingdom is not of this world" (John 18:36). However, the Jewish leaders were quite right in thinking that:

• He would come from heaven.

• He would exist for ages prior to his coming.

• He would eventually establish the Kingdom of God.

• He would rule over it forever.

Various prophecies foretold Jesus' rejection by the Jews (Psalm 118:22 and Isaiah 8:14). Jesus referred to Psalm 118:22 when He spoke of being rejected by His own people, as stated in Matthew 21:42 and Mark 12:10-11. We read of the fulfillment of this prophecy in 1 Peter 2:7 and Romans 9:32-33.

ANNOUNCING THE AWESOME GOOD NEWS

An angel appeared to a group of shepherds in the fields of Bethlehem, and the glory of the Lord shone around them, and the angel made this wonderful proclamation: "'Do not be afraid. I bring you good news of great joy that will be for all the people. Today in the town of David a Savior has been born to you; he is Christ the Lord. This will be a sign to you: You will find a baby wrapped in cloths and lying in a manger.' Suddenly a great company of the heavenly host appeared with the angel, praising God and saying, 'Glory to God in the highest, and on earth peace to men on whom his favor rests'" (Luke 2:8-13). What a great moment this was in the history of humanity. AL-Masih who was to be the Savior and Ruler over all people had finally arrived.

For this reason God's Word tells us that his birth is "Good News."

AGREEMENT ON THE "GOOD NEWS"

It is a fact that the Qur'an agrees with the Gospel regarding the identity of the Messiah. According to both of them, Jesus, the Son of Mary, is the Messiah. It is very interesting to observe that the Qur'an not only agrees with the Bible that AL-Masih, the Messiah, is Jesus, the son of Mary, but the Qur'an also confirms the Biblical fact that Jesus' birth is Good News. It declares in Surah 3:45: "Behold! The angel said: 'O Mary! Allah giveth thee Glad Tidings of a Word from Him: His name will be Christ Jesus the son of Mary, held in honor in this world and the hereafter and of (the company of) those Nearest to Allah.' "[32]

Many people in the world have never heard or understood why God declared the birth of the Messiah to be Good News. Of course Satan (Shaitan) does not want anyone to know about the "Glad Tidings" of God for humanity. We read in 2 Corinthians 4:3-6: "And even if our gospel is veiled, it is veiled to those who are perishing. The god of this age has blinded the minds of unbelievers, so that they cannot see the light of the gospel of the glory of Christ, who is the image of God. For we do not preach ourselves, but Jesus Christ as Lord, and ourselves as your servants for Jesus' sake. For God, who said, 'Let light shine out of darkness,' made his light shine in our hearts to give us the light of the knowledge of the glory of God in the face of Christ." The "god of this age" is Satan.

IDENTITY OF JESUS

We learn from the Scripture that Jesus, AL-Masih, is the revelation of God's mercy, love and salvation to humanity. It is very clear in the Scripture that the coming Messiah would be nothing less than the Son of God and the Savior of the world. However, when Jesus appeared among the people, He was received with mixed reaction. Many people rejected Him. Some thought of Him as just a prophet. And others disputed His identity. For example, the High Priest of the Jews said to Jesus, "I charge you under oath by the living God: tell us if you are the Christ, the Son of God" (Matthew 26:63).

There were many people who recognized Jesus as "the Messiah," "the Anointed One," and who followed Him. We read the following accounts from the Gospel:

"When Jesus came to the region of Caesarea Philippi, he asked his disciples, 'Who do people say the Son of Man is?' They replied, 'Some say John the Baptist; others say Elijah; and still others, Jeremiah or one of the prophets.' 'But what about you?' he asked. 'Who do you say I am?' Simon Peter answered, 'You are the Christ, the Son of the living God.' " (Matthew 16:13-16)

Martha said, "'Yes, Lord,' she told him, 'I believe that you are the Christ, the Son of God, who was to come into the world.' " (John 11:27)

MIRACULOUS SIGNS AND WONDERS

During His mission on earth, Christ Jesus displayed great power and authority as no one had ever done before that time. This was a definite sign confirming that He was truly the Anointed One sent by God to be the Savior and Ruler of the world. We read in the Bible:

> "Jesus did many other miraculous signs in the presence of his disciples, which are not recorded in this book. But these are written that you may believe that Jesus is the Christ, the Son of God, and that by believing you may have life in his name" (John 20:30-31).

> "You know what has happened throughout Judea, beginning in Galilee after the baptism that John [Yahya] preached — how God anointed Jesus of Nazareth with the Holy Spirit and power, and how he went around doing good and healing all who were under the power of the devil, because God was with him" (Acts 10:37-38).

The Qur'an says that the miracles performed by Jesus were "clear Signs" of God's power. These clear signs were not granted to all of the prophets. The Qur'an states in Surah 2:253, "Those Messengers we endowed with gifts, some above others: ...To Jesus, the son of Mary, we gave clear (Signs)..." Commenting on this verse, AL-Baidawi said: "God made Jesus' miracles the evidence of his preferment (above all the prophets) because they are clear signs and great miracles. Together those miracles were not performed by anyone else."[33]

In Surah 3:49 we read: "...I have come to you, with a Sign from your Lord, in that I make for you out of clay, as it were, the figure of a bird, and breathe into it, and it becomes a bird by Allah's leave. And I heal those born blind, and the lepers, and I quicken the dead, by Allah's leave; and I declare to you what ye eat, and what ye store in your houses. Surely therein is a Sign for you if ye did believe."

In the Gospel, Luke 6:17-19, we read that a great multitude of people had come to hear Jesus and to be healed of their diseases. "He went down with them and stood on a level place. A large crowd of his disciples was there and a great number of people from all over Judea, from Jerusalem, and from the coast of Tyre and Sidon, who had come to hear him and to be healed of their diseases. Those troubled by evil spirits were cured..." Jesus alone displayed the Great Power of God, and Jesus alone is able to heal those who believe in Him from their diseases.

It is surprising, and no doubt disappointing to many Muslim scholars, that the Qur'an never states that Muhammad performed any miracle or signs. In fact, Surah 28:48 even addresses this absence, stating: "But (now), when the Truth has come to them from Ourselves, They say, "Why are not (Signs) sent to him, like Those which were sent to Moses?"

CHAPTER 11

JESUS CHRIST, "HIS WORD" (KALIMATUHUU)

Jesus is called "His Word" (Kalimatuhuu) which simply means, The Word of God. Surah 4:171 reads: "...Christ Jesus the son of Mary...and His Word..."

In Surah 3:45, we also read what the angel said to Mary, "...Allah giveth thee Glad tidings of a Word from Him: his name will be Christ Jesus the Son of Mary..."

In Surah 3:39, Jesus is called "a word from Allah" when the angel announces to Zachariah that his son Yahya (John the Baptist) will witness the truth of a Word from God. Clearly, the Qur'an agrees with the Gospel that John the Baptist (Prophet Yahya) proclaimed "The Word" (Kalima) from God. According to the Gospel, in Matthew 2:11, 12 and John 1:23-27, John was sent by God to prepare the way and announce the coming of the Messiah.

In the Qur'an and the Gospel, Jesus is the only person who is given this title. In Revelation 19:13, Jesus is called the Word of God, "He is dressed in a robe dipped in blood, and his name is the Word of God." We can clearly see the emphasis of deity in this title. Have you noticed this, my friend? Jesus, himself in His actual person is the Word, and the source and origin of the Word is God. The Qur'an gives no explanation for this title.

Since God Himself calls Jesus The Word of God, it is clear that Jesus in his own person must be the one and only perfect expression of God's mind and will. This is what the Gospel tells us in Colossians 1:15-19, "He is the image of the invisible God..."

The Word of God is One who indeed is actively the real revelation of God to men. To know Him is to know God, and this is what Jesus said in John 14:9, "...Anyone who has seen me has seen the Father..." Jesus does not merely bring the revelation and words of God to men; rather, he Himself is that very Word which came from heaven to earth.

THE NATURE OF THE WORD OF GOD

Jesus is the Word of God and since the Word of God is eternal and uncreated, it follows that God, the Father, and His Word, Jesus, are one. If someone states that they are not One, then that person is saying that there are two separate entities who have existed from all eternity. That is blasphemy because only one God is eternal. Someone who says that the "Word of God" was created and therefore is not eternal is equivalent to saying there was a time when God was unable to speak and then later He did. This would violate the doctrine that God is unchangeable.

We find a clear explanation of the title that is given to Jesus in the Qur'an and the Gospel: In the Gospel according to John 1:1-4, "In the beginning was the Word, and the Word was with God, and the Word was God. He was with God in the beginning. Through him all things were made; without him nothing was made that has been made. In him was life, and that life was the light of men."

The Gospel teaches us that in the beginning before God ever began to create, the Word already existed. Jesus always was throughout all eternity the Word of God. The very nature of the Word is that of God. Jesus alone is the Word of God and is therefore the sole means of communication between God and His creatures.

The teaching of the Gospel as recorded by John is that Jesus existed as the Word of God before God ever created anything. Therefore, He is deity. The Word of God became the man Christ Jesus, the son of Mary. John 1:14 reveals: "The Word became flesh and made his dwelling among us. We have seen his glory, the glory of the One and Only, who came from the Father, full of grace and truth." When we are told that the Word became flesh, this does not mean that the Word or Logos ceased to be what He was. The verb "egeneto" in John 1:14 (The Word became flesh) certainly does not mean that the Logos changed into flesh (or "sarx") and thus altered His essential nature. It means that He took on that particular characteristic. He acquired an additional form without in any way changing his essential nature. He remained the infinite and unchangeable Son of God. The word "sarx" (flesh) here denotes human nature.

We read in Hebrews 1:1-3: "In the past God spoke to our forefathers through the prophets at many times and in various ways, but in these last days he has spoken to us by his Son... The Son is the radiance of God's glory and the exact representation of his being..." We have in Jesus the fullest possible expression of God to man. It was through Jesus that God expressed fully His character and communicated with us. "In Him was life, and that life was the light of men" (John 1:4). Our Muslim brothers fail to make this link between the Word and life. God's Word is infinitely different from our word.

It is interesting that an eminent Muslim scholar, Dr. Qaradawi, wrote: "If our hearing is through the sense of hearing that gets transmitted by air, God's hearing differs from ours. And if our sight comprehends things through the sense of seeing, and the rays (of light), God's seeing is not like ours."[34] The Qur'an states in Surah 42:11: "...there is nothing whatever like unto Him..."

CHRIST IS LIKE "THE BOOK OF GOD"

In Surah 3:39, Jesus is called "a Word from God." AL-Baidawi, one of the famous Muslim scholars, commented on Surah 3:39: "Jesus is called the Word of God because he is like the Book of God. This is a very significant statement. According to the teaching of Muslim scholars and the Muslim beliefs, the book of God, the Qur'an, which is recited by tongues, written in books (Masahif), and remembered in hearts, is eternal and exists in God Himself. It cannot be separated or parted from God by transferring it to the hearts or by writing it on paper.[35]

My dear Muslim friend, Jesus' inner being proceeds from God and is still in God's innermost. It is exactly as AL-Baidawi said, "Christ is like the Book of God," and as the Qur'an said, "Christ is God's Word."

Perhaps by understanding the relation of God to His Word, we can better understand the relation of Jesus as Son to His Father in the unity of God. Both Christians and Muslims agree that God is eternal, God's Word is eternal, and that God is one. Both believe that God has bridged the gulf between the infinite and finite by revealing His eternal Word to His finite creation. Muslims believe that God expresses His eternal word to His created world through the Book called the Qur'an. For Muslims the Word resides eternally both within the being of God and within the pages of the Arabic Qur'an. Muslims further believe that the Qur'an was revealed to Muhammad at a particular place and time, almost fourteen centuries ago. For the Muslim believer, the infinite and the finite meet within the Arabic Qur'an.

In Christianity, God communicated His eternal Word to His created world through a person called Jesus. For this reason the Bible speaks of the eternal Word of God becoming flesh in the man, Jesus. As Jesus is called the eternal Word of God, so He is called the eternal Son of God. Before the eternal Word or Son became the man Jesus (and before Mary was born), the Word or Son was residing eternally in the being of God. Jesus (the Messiah) is the eternal living Word of God in human form.

CAN THE WORD OF GOD BE CREATED?

Muslims believe that God's uncreated Word (uncreated like God Himself), can become a created book, namely (the Arabic Qur'an). Prominent Scholar Ibn Hazm reports the leading scholar Ibn Hanbal as saying, "the Word of God is His eternal knowledge and hence it is uncreated."[36] Muslim scholars agree that the Qur'an has two aspects (natures)— human and divine. They claim:

- It has the human (physical) nature because it is written in books by human hands, it appeared in human history, and it is subject to wear and tear.

- It has the divine nature because the Qur'an is the knowledge of God. It exists in God Himself and cannot be separated and parted from God by writing it on papers. Thus it is eternal.

Significantly, one of the early leaders of the Muslim world, Caliph Ma'moun (786-833 A.D.), resisted the belief that the Qur'an is uncreated. He wrote in a letter to the Governor of Baghdad stating that those who believe that the Qur'an is uncreated are "like Christians when they claim that Jesus the Son of Mary was not created because he was the Word of God."[37]

My dear Muslim friend, I pray that you will see that God, motivated by His strong love for "spiritually sick" mankind, was not satisfied to send only a book. He chose to present Himself as our personal Physician and Savior in the person of Jesus.

Please allow me to illustrate. Imagine a man in desperation sinking in the ocean. He can barely keep his head above water. If you were that man, which would be your urgent need: for someone to throw you a book of swimming instructions, or for someone to dive in the water and rescue you? In the Gospel, God told us that the human race is sinking in the mud of sin and He came to save us!

CHAPTER 12
JESUS CHRIST, "A SPIRIT FROM GOD" (RUHUN MINHU)

Surah 4:171 states, "...Christ Jesus the son of Mary...and a Spirit proceeding from Him [Ruhun Minhu]..." In another well-accepted translation of the Qur'an the term "Ruhun Minhu" is translated as "A Spirit From God."

In the Qur'an, Jesus is the only one who is given the title "Spirit from God." God again is the source of the Spirit as He is the source of the Word. This title is not explained in the Qur'an. It is clear that this title supports the Christian belief that Jesus was not a creature made from dust but an eternal Spirit who took on human flesh.

The Qur'an tells us that Jesus, the Messiah, Son of Mary, is "a Spirit from God." This statement affirms the pre-existence of Jesus before His conception on earth. In Islamic *Traditions* (Hadith), which is a record of the words and deeds of Muhammad, Jesus is referred to as a "Spirit of God."

Jesus is God's Spirit. In AL-AHadith AL-Qudsiyyah, we read "Jesus, the servant of Allah, His Apostle, His Word and His Spirit."[38] In the introduction of this same book, the author highlights the authority of the *AL-Ahadith AL-Qudsiyyah* as follows: "Hadith Qudsi, however, is a report of what God said, though not necessarily in His words. The Divine authority, explicitly stated or implicit in the context of the Hadith Qudsi, gives this group of Hadith a special character and significance to Muslims and non-Muslims alike."

AL-Baidawi, in his comments on Surah 4:171, said: "Jesus was called 'Spirit' because he used to raise dead bodies and dead hearts to life."[39]

The Qur'an refers many times to the "Holy Spirit," as in Surah 2:87 and Surah 2:253. We read in Surah 16:102: "Say, the Holy Spirit has brought the revelation from thy Lord in Truth, in order to strengthen those who believe and as a Guide and Glad Tidings to Muslims." It is presumed that the Holy Spirit comes from heaven and is purely a Spirit. In Surah 4:171, Jesus is called "a Spirit proceeding from Him" (Ruhun Minhu). The same exact expression is used again in Surah 58:22 where it is said that God strengthens true believers with "a Spirit from Himself" (Ruhun Minhu).

Abdullah Yusuf Ali defines the term "Spirit from God" in his internationally acclaimed translation and commentary, *The Meaning of the Holy Qur'an*. He commented on Surah 58:22, "The phrase used here is stronger, 'a spirit from Himself.' " He inferred that "The Spirit from God" is greater than "The Holy Spirit." In explaining what "Spirit from God" means, he said it is "...the Divine Spirit, which we can no more define adequately than we can define in human language the nature and attributes of Allah."[40] This is an amazing comment which clearly and strongly indicates that "a Spirit from Him" is the very Spirit of the Living God, uncreated and eternal in essence.

Abdullah Yusuf Ali says it is, "the divine Spirit which we can no more define adequately than we can define in human language the nature and attributes of God."

The words scholar Ali used in his commentary are not vague. A "Spirit from God" is clearly believed by him to be from the realm of Deity and not from the created order. "Spirit from God" is the very title that the Qur'an gives to Jesus in Surah 4:171. Abdullah Yusuf Ali's interpretation of the term "Spirit from God" in Surah 58:22, can only lead us to conclude that Jesus is the Divine Spirit whom we can no more define adequately in human language than we can define the very nature and attributes of God. My dear Muslim friend, the exact same words are used. Jesus is the "Ruhun-Minhu, a Spirit from God." He is, therefore, God in essence and nature. Jesus is God who appeared in the flesh.

The belief that Jesus is the Word of Allah and a Spirit from him is, in some traditions, called a requirement for admission into Paradise:

> Ubade ibn Samit comments that Muhammad, the prophet of Islam, said, "Whoever attests that there is no God but Allah, that Muhammad is his slave and ambassador, that Jesus is his slave, prophet, and word which he placed in Mary — and that he is a spirit from him — and whoever confesses that heaven and hell exist, him will Allah allow to enter Paradise according to his deeds."[41]

CHAPTER 13

GOD RANSOMED ABRAHAM'S SON

We read in the Qur'an the story of the prophet Abraham. God had instructed Abraham to sacrifice his son. As he was about to perform the sacrifice, God intervened. We read these significant words in the Qur'an, in Surah 37:104-107: "We called out to him, 'O Abraham! Thou hast already fulfilled the vision'... and We ransomed him (Abraham's son) with a momentous sacrifice.."[42]

My Muslim friend, in the story of Abraham recorded in the Qur'an, Surah 37, Abraham was going to sacrifice his son but God set his son free. However, did God simply allow the prophet Abraham to take his son and leave? No, a sacrificial offering was still required. The only way that Abraham's son could be freed was by substituting another sacrifice. God loved Abraham's son; therefore, He rescued him and ransomed him. God provided the sacrifice to be offered in his place. Note that God was the one who provided the alternate sacrifice. We read in Surah 37:107 these significant words: "...and We ransomed him (Abraham's son) with a momentous sacrifice." It was God, who ransomed us by a sacrifice that He Himself provided.

Jesus (AL-Masih Isa) is the One about whom the prophet Yahya (John the Baptist) proclaimed in John 1:29, "...Look, the Lamb of God, who takes away the sin of the world!" The prophet Isaiah, inspired of God, spoke of the Messiah as a sacrificial lamb. "He was oppressed and afflicted, yet he did not open his mouth; he was led like a lamb to the slaughter, and as a sheep before her shearers is silent, so he did not open his mouth" (Isaiah 53:7). Surah 37:107 states, "and we ransomed him with a momentous sacrifice." What was described in this verse as "a momentous sacrifice" was also translated "mighty sacrifice" and "valuable beyond estimation" in other universally recognized translations of the Qur'an.

The logical question is: What kind of sacrifice is this that deserves to be called "momentous," "mighty," and "valuable beyond estimation?" Obviously, the ram that Abraham found in the bushes is not the one intended to fit this description. The answer is very clear in the Bible in 1 Peter 1:18-19: "For you know that it was not with perishable things such as silver or gold that you were redeemed"[43] from the empty way of life handed down to you from your forefathers, but with the precious blood of Christ, a lamb without blemish or defect."

"If salvation is only a matter of rewarding those who do good, and if God's purpose was only to test Abraham's obedience, why then was there a need for a "momentous sacrifice"? Was it not sufficient that Abraham went as far as he did?"[44]

The Gospel tells us that because God loves us so much, He rescued us through the ultimate sacrifice ("valuable beyond estimation" and "momentous") of His Word, Isa, the Messiah whom the Qur'an describes as "a Spirit proceeding from God." AL-Masih Isa took our place and was sacrificed on our behalf. He died on the cross to free us from the penalty of our sins, which is eternal separation from God.

Jesus Christ is the one whom the prophet Yahya (John the Baptist) proclaimed in Injeel, John 1:29: "Look, the lamb of God who takes away the sins of the world." The most valuable sacrifice that God could give is of Himself. For this reason He came to our world in the person of Jesus to save us.

WHO WILL PROVIDE OUR RANSOM?

In Surah 10:54, we read, "Every soul that hath sinned, If it possessed all That is on earth, would fain give it in ransom..." A ransom is the required price to pay for the release of a captive. God is the only one able to provide a ransom for our freedom.

In the Torah God commanded the people to sacrifice an animal, such as a lamb, sheep or a goat which had no flaw or blemish. The animal was brought to the priest who would lay his hands on its head and confess the sins of the person who brought the animal. The sins were thereby transferred onto the animal, which was slain by the priest who slit its throat. The priest would then spread upon the altar the animal's blood so that there might be the remission of sin. Thus the penalty for sin, which is death, was paid by the animal's death as a substitute for the person.

Leviticus 17:11 tells us, "For the life of a creature is in the blood, and I have given it to you to make atonement for yourselves on the altar; it is the blood that makes atonement for one's life." This is the significance of the Cross, my dear Muslim friend. Life for life. Christ sacrificed his life in order to give us the right to live forever and to be free from paying the penalty for our sins. We read in Matthew 20:28, "Just as the Son of Man did not come to be served, but to serve, and to give his life as a ransom for many."

The Muslims celebrate an annual feast called Feast of Sacrifice (Id AL-Adha). On this day, animals are sacrificed. The Muslim world generally believes that this festival commemorates the willingness of Abraham to offer his son as a sacrifice to God.

Traditions tells us that Muhammad himself offered sacrifices during this festival. Muhammad offered two rams on the day of the Festival of Sacrifice and offered a prayer in which he said, "O God, this sacrifice is of thee and for thee; accept it from Muhammad and his people."[45] Although the sacrifices on Id AL-Adha are considered generally by Muslims to be commemorative, some traditions and beliefs about them indicate awareness of a deeper significance to the festival showing that the shed blood of the sacrifice is very significant. Ayisha relates that the prophet said, "Man has not done anything, on the day of sacrifice more pleasing to God than spilling blood, for verily the animal sacrificed will come on the Day of Resurrection...and will make the scales of his action heavy. Verily its blood reacheth the acceptance of God before it falleth upon the ground, therefore be joyful in it."[46] Here is the recognition of the Biblical principle, life for life. In the Old Testament when a person sinned, he forfeited his right to live. He was allowed to continue to live because an animal's life was offered as a substitution for him.

Hebrews 9:22 reads: "In fact, the law requires that nearly everything be cleansed with blood, and without the shedding of blood there is no forgiveness." A life for life. Christ forfeited His life in order to give us the right to live. Ephesians 1:7-9 reads: "In him we have redemption through his blood, the forgiveness of sins, in accordance with the riches of God's grace that he lavished on us with all wisdom and understanding. And he made known to us the mystery of his will according to his good pleasure, which he purposed in Christ..."

Jesus came to pay a debt He didn't owe because we owed a debt we couldn't pay. I am reminded of a true story about Shamuel, the Caucasian Prince. He lived about two hundred years ago. His people were constantly at war with the Turks. One night, he planned a surprised attack but his enemy was waiting. His secret plans had been revealed to the enemy and many of his soldiers lost their lives. Ultimately, he lost the battle. Shamuel announced the traitor would be punished with one hundred lashes of the whip. In great secrecy Shamuel's army launched another attack but the same thing happened. His enemy was waiting. They lost another battle but discovered the traitor. It was Shamuel's mother.

What should Shamuel do? What a difficult question. If he exempted his mother from punishment, his followers would say that he was unjust. They would be correct. The alternative would be even more difficult. How could he mandate the painful punishment and perhaps death of his beloved mother?

Shamuel addressed his people. "We lost two battles because of treason. Many of our men were killed. There is no excuse — the crime was committed and punishment shall be executed according to my judgment — ONE HUNDRED LASHES! Righteousness and justice must be maintained."

His mother was filled with fear as she was led away to the circle where punishment would be administered. The executioner lifted his whip. But before the first blow was delivered, Shamuel shouted out, "Wait — she is my mother, I will take the punishment for her." He removed his clothes and commanded, "Executioner, you dare not strike me with less force than you would have my mother. I am the person who will take her punishment. Do your duty — Strike on!" Lash after lash was laid on the back of Shamuel until he collapsed to the ground unconscious. He survived the lashing in spite of all expectations.

Jesus came to liberate us from the kingdom of Satan (Shaitan). He came to save the world from the judgment of sin. The well known Muslim scholar, Qasemi, in his famous commentary, Mahasen at-Ta'aweel, commented on Surah 3:45: "The name Isa is an Arabic form from a Greek word, which means Savior and it is equivalent to Joshua in Hebrew." In the Gospel, Matthew 1:21 states: "She [Mary] will give birth to a son, and you [Joseph] are to give him the name Jesus, because he will save his people from their sins."

HIS SACRIFICE AND OUR JUSTIFICATION

We know from the Hadith that Muhammad told his daughter Fatima, "Be present, oh Fatima, at the head of the victim for as soon as the first drop of blood falls to the ground your sins will be forgiven."

Of course these animals that were sacrificed in Old Testament times were not equal in value to the souls for whom they were offered. In fact any one person was more valuable and precious than all of the animals offered. These sacrifices were symbolic of the valuable sacrifice of Christ. This is the only sacrifice which God could accept as equal to the souls of all mankind.

God promises to justify and declare righteous any sinner who believes that Jesus died for his sins at the cross. The moment the sinner believes in Jesus as his Savior, all of his sins are forgiven, removed and he is reconciled with God (Romans 5:1). The sinner will no longer be separated from God.

It is a gift by God's grace that justifies the sinner who believes. Justification by faith means God is declaring believers to be righteous not on the basis of their own works but on the basis of their faith and trust in Christ's sacrifice. God declares that He has accepted the sacrifice of Christ as the payment of our debt according to divine justice. Relying on our own works can only condemn us. My dear reader allow me to ask you, what does God see when He looks at you? Does He see religious deeds mixed with sin or does He see His own righteousness imparted to you through your faith in Christ. This is the only standard of righteousness that He accepts.

I remember when I was a child I would on occasion get into trouble. My father owned the building in which we lived in Egypt and his legal practice was on the ground floor while we lived upstairs. Many times I invited my friends over to play soccer and we played inside the hallway of the building. One time the ball hit the light bulb and another time it hit one of my father's clients. On occasion the ball hit the glass door of my father's office causing a great disturbance to his business conversations. Not to mention the joyful yelling and screaming when I scored a goal. When my father finished work and came home he would give me that certain look that told me, I was in trouble. I would run to my mother crying and hide behind her asking for forgiveness. Many times when my father came home, even though he was angry, he would see my mother's beautiful face and my repentant heart and let me go unpunished. Other times, my mother would gather me in her arms and shield me with her body so that when my father would reach out to punish me, his hand would fall on her instead of me. This memory always reminds me of when I ran to Jesus in 1976, He covered me with His righteousness and God forgave all of my sins.

The moment you receive Jesus Christ as *your* Lord and Savior, God declares your sins to have been washed away by the blood of the cross. He credits the righteousness of Christ to your account.

However, the free forgiveness of sin that the Christian enjoys does not give the Christian the right to continue to sin freely. No true Christian will purposely continue in his sin. In Romans 6:15-18, Paul the Apostle says: "What then? Shall we sin because we are not under law but under grace? By no means! Don't you know that when you offer yourselves to someone to obey him as slaves, you are slaves to the one whom you obey — whether you are slaves to sin, which leads to death, or to obedience, which leads to righteousness?

But thanks be to God that, though you used to be slaves to sin, you wholeheartedly obeyed the form of teaching to which you were entrusted. You have been set free from sin and have become slaves to righteousness."

Christ gives his true followers the power to will and to do good. Titus 2:14 reads: "[Jesus] who gave himself for us to redeem us from all wickedness and to purify for himself a people that are his very own, eager to do what is good."

SECTION FIVE

WHY WAS JESUS NECESSARY?

CHAPTER 14
THE PROBLEM OF SIN

Because sin is found in every human heart, there is no doubt that everyone needs salvation. According to the Hadith, the sinfulness of all human beings is confirmed. The Hadith says that: "Satan circulates in the human mind as blood circulates in it." Muhammad, the prophet Islam, also said: "Shaitan runs in the body of Adam's son (man) as his blood circulates in it."[47] The Qur'an attributes sin to all the prophets except Jesus! According to the Bible, Romans 3:23, "For all have sinned..." The Qur'an in Surah 12:53 says, "...The (human) soul is certainly prone to evil..." We read in Surah 14:34, "Verily, man is given up to injustice and ingratitude." Surah 100:6 says, "Truly man is to his Lord, ungrateful."

My dear Muslim friend, the sin that is found in us manifests itself often in our thoughts, actions and words. This makes us impure before God. For example: At the market you are given a choice of three meat mixtures. The first has 50% beef and 50% pork. The next has 90% beef and 10% pork. The third has 99% beef and 1% pork. Which one will you buy? As a devout Muslim you would refuse them all. Any amount of pork, no matter how insignificant makes the meat "Haram" (unlawful to eat). That is how sin is. Any sin in us (even what we think of as a small sin) puts us in a state of defiance to His will and to Him as Lord, thus we become *unacceptable* in God's eyes! It makes us unable to obtain holy God's approval and favor and will leave us unworthy to enter Paradise.

According to the Islamic teaching and beliefs, if you washed all your body in preparation to pray but before you started your prayer some dirt fell on you, ritually you would be considered unclean. God would not accept your prayers. If you believed that some dirt on your physical body disqualified you from praying, it shouldn't be too difficult to accept the fact that the dirt of sin within you would make you unclean before God.

If a husband slept with a woman other than his wife even once, he would be considered unfaithful. No wife would accept partial fidelity from her husband. In the same way God considers our partial obedience as disobedience which He can not accept.

My dear Muslim friend, would you accept a glass of water if I added one drop of ink to it? You would most likely refuse. In the same way the pure, just and holy God can not accept us into heaven on the basis of our good works. Our lives contain many black, evil, impure, selfish, and sinful deeds which good works cannot erase. God will not allow any defiled or impure person to enter Paradise.

Remember what the Qur'an says about Hell fire in Surah 19:71 which states, "Not one of you but will pass over it: this is, with Thy Lord, a Decree which must be accomplished." In a different translation of the Qur'an to the same verse, we read the expression "pass through it" instead of "pass over it." People ask whether this verse refers to the wicked or includes all men? What is meant by the phrase "passing through it"? In AL-Itqan[48] the Suyuti tells us that Muhammad himself has answered this question and said, "there is no righteous or debaucher who would not enter hell."

Likewise, the famous Muslim scholar and religious figure Sheikh Kishk reinforces Suyuti's statement.[49]

Tragically, according to the Qur'an and the Hadith, no Muslim can be sure of what to expect after death. The God of the Qur'an does not guarantee the Muslim believer forgiveness of his sins, acceptance, or a promise of eternal life. For example, Abu Bakr AL-Sadik, the first Caliph, is regarded by all Muslims as one of the best Muslims. Even Muhammad acknowledged that Abu Bakr AL-Sadik was the closest to him and he told the believers to emulate Abu Bakr AL-Sadik as an example. Therefore the Muslims elected him as Caliph after the death of Muhammad.

Abu Bakr always believed in Muhammad and in all that he uttered. He obeyed him blindly. As Muhammad was suffering from a sickness which ultimately caused his death, he ordered Abu Bakr to lead the Muslims in prayer. What did Abu Bakr AL-Sadik say about God? "I swear to God that I do not feel safe from God's cunning (deceitfulness) even if one of my feet is already inside paradise."[50]

What an acknowledgment spoken by Abu Bakr, "...I do not feel safe from God's cunning even if one of my feet is already inside paradise." Maybe he feared his God would deceive him and push that foot outside of Paradise because He changed His mind. There is no other meaning of this statement. Abu Bakr Al Sadik said, when resurrection, Paradise, and Hell were mentioned in his presence, "I wish I were a tree eaten by an animal; I wish I had never been born."[51] Obviously, he was frightened by God.

This is not surprising because God in Islam, according to the words of the Qur'an and Muhammad, does not bestow on the believer any assurance concerning eternity.

WHAT SHOULD THE JUDGE DO?

Since God is holy, our sins must be an insult to God and harmful to man whom God created and loved. Thus the sinner deserves the judgment of God. God is not just unless He punishes the sinner. Repentance alone, which is a return to the place of obedience, cannot remove past sins. It cannot satisfy the holiness and justice of God even if we add our good works to it.

My Muslim friend, please allow me to give you an example. Imagine that a young man is brought before the judge for rape. The man pleads, "I repent and I am very sorry for what I did and I will never do it again. Your Honor, I promise to be nice, gentle and sensitive to all the women I meet for the rest of my life. I will help my neighbor, an old woman, clean her house. I will donate much of my time and money to help victims of rape. As a matter of fact, Your Honor, I can prove that I did many, many good deeds before and after this crime. Your Honor, I am really sorry for the wrong I did to this woman and I am sorry I broke the law. Since I have done many good deeds and I plan to do more, I am asking you to grant to me a pardon. Forgive me for raping this woman and set me free." How do you think the judge should respond? You would most likely agree that the judge would doubtless respond, "Although I appreciate your good deeds, I must deal with your crime and punish you."

My beloved Muslim reader, it will be the same when we stand before God on the day of judgment. Because of His holiness and justice (righteousness), He has to deal with our sins. Eternal punishment is certain for those whose sins are not forgiven. The truth is that repentance and good works do not eradicate the effect of sin or guilt. We are required to do good works, but we cannot use them to offset our bad deeds. Good works are a requirement, not a solution. There is nothing that man himself can do to prevent the judgment of God. Yet God's justice demands that the penalty for sin be paid. Since we are the ones who have sinned, we must pay the penalty.

The Good News is that The Messiah, Jesus, has paid the price for us with the shed blood of His sacrificial death. The Cross of Christ reveals God's judgment on sin. What Christ accomplished on the cross fulfilled the demands of the Law of God. There was in Jesus' sufferings and substitutionary death an atonement, which justifies the sinner who believes and repents. "He [AL-Masih] is the atoning sacrifice for our sins, and not only for ours but also for the sins of the whole world" (1 John 2:2).

Christ broke down the barrier between man and God. "This is love: not that we loved God, but that he loved us and sent his Son as an atoning sacrifice for our sins" (1 John 4:10). The sinner will be saved immediately if he accepts by faith this truth as a gift of mercy and grace from God. In the Bible, Acts 10:43 says: "All the prophets testify about him that everyone who believes in him receives forgiveness of sins through his name."

Remember, my friend, that none of us can say with a clear conscience, I am not a sinner. If we sin only a few times a day, that would add up to tens of thousands of sins by the end of our lives. The fantastic news is that the Gospel dealt clearly with our problem of sin and provided the solution for it. "For all have sinned and fall short of the glory of God, and are justified freely by his grace through the redemption that came by Christ Jesus" (Romans 3:23-24). We can only be considered pure by the grace and mercy of God. Surah 24:21 recounts: "...and were it not for the grace and mercy of Allah on you, not one of you would ever have been pure ..."

God knows that we are unable to save ourselves, and because of His deep and amazing love towards us He offers to give us salvation as a free gift. "For it is by grace you have been saved, through faith — and this not from yourselves, it is the gift of God — not by works, so that no one can boast" (Ephesians 2:8-9).

God wants you to obtain and enjoy His salvation. He wants to give you salvation as a gift. If you tried to earn it by your efforts you could not because you do not deserve it. But if you ask God to save you, He will because He loves you. This story will demonstrate: Once there was a poor woman who earnestly needed some fruit from the king's garden for her and her family. She tried to pay the king's gardener money for the fruit, but he refused the money. Each time she attempted to buy the fruit, her offer was refused. The woman pleaded with the gardener to take her money. The prince, the king's son, heard the woman's begging. After he had learned what was happening, the kind prince told the woman, "My father is not a merchant but he is the king. He owns everything you see. He does not need your money. You cannot buy his fruit, but he will give it freely to you if you ask sincerely. The prince picked some fruit and gave to the woman all she needed.

CHAPTER 15

GOD HIMSELF CAME TO US IN THE PERSON OF THE MESSIAH

Many Muslims will say, "How can God be found in a man in the person of the Messiah?" My dear Muslim reader, God can show Himself to people in different ways. For example, God showed Himself to Moses in a burning bush. For we read in Surah 27:7-9: "Behold! Moses said to his family: I perceive a fire...But when he came to the (Fire), a voice was heard: ... Glory to Allah, the Lord of the Worlds. O Moses! Verily, I am Allah, the Exalted in Might, the Wise!..." In the Torah we read in Exodus 3:4: "When the LORD saw that he had gone over to look, God called to him from within the bush, 'Moses! Moses!' And Moses said, 'Here I am.' " God manifested Himself in the fire to speak to Moses.

The Gospel teaches us that God chose to enter our world by being conceived through the Holy Spirit in the body of a virgin. God in the person of Jesus Christ chose to dwell in a human body. Even in this earthly form He remained pure and sinless as He expressed His wonderful love for the human race.

I am also aware that many Muslims comment on the fact that Jesus ate, drank and slept at night when He lived on earth. Therefore they wonder, "How can He be God? God does not *need* to do any of these things that humans do."

It is true that God didn't have to do any of these things. A king also does not have to sleep where the servants in his kingdom sleep. He does not have to eat

119

with them or share their food. He certainly does not
have to go through these humbling experiences but he
can *choose* to do so. If he wants to get close to them and
experience their feelings and ultimately solve their
problems, he will spend time with them in their environment. The king can also wear the clothes of the sol-
dier and remain the king. This is our God, the servant-
King and the soldier-King. The Bible tells us, "For you
know the grace of our Lord Jesus Christ, that though
he was rich, yet for your sakes he became poor, so that
you through his poverty might become rich" (2
Corinthians 8:9).

My dear friends, who among us would dare to place
limitations upon God's power and will? Are we not lim-
iting God by saying that He is unable to express
Himself through human form? Man cannot become
God, but God can manifest Himself through the perfect
man, Jesus Christ.

Remember that the Qur'an also tells us that the
Spirit of God can appear in human form. We have an
example of this fact in Surah 19:17: "...We sent to her
Our angel, and he appeared before her as a man in all
respects." The original Arabic text does not state "Our
angel," but rather "Ruhana." It should be translated,
"...We sent to her Our Spirit." "Our Spirit" not "Our
angel" is the correct translation to the Arabic word
"Ruhana." The Bible and the Qur'an acknowledge that
God sends His angels, who are spirit in form (ruh), in
the exact likeness of human appearance. There is no
reasonable argument against the possibility of the Son
of God, who is likewise Spirit in form, to take actual
human form.

Many Muslim scholars such as Assfy say, "God does not have to be associated in any way with men."[52] In the Gospel God revealed Himself as the God who desires to meet us at our level and graciously identify Himself very closely with us. He is the God who longs for us to go to Him so He can embrace us and indwell us with His Spirit. He wants to adopt us as children and becomes our Father.

The Qur'an states in Surah 55:14, "He created man from...clay like unto pottery." This verse indicates that God stood on earth at a definite time and place. He made Adam at a specific time by holding in His hand clay from a specific spot of the earth. Nonetheless, His standing at a specific place and time does not confine Him because God is Almighty. In the same way, my dear friend, God's incarnation (coming in the form of a man) at a specific time and place does not confine Him because God is Almighty and Omnipresent.

THE BEST WAY GOD COULD HAVE COMMUNICATED TO HUMANITY

We should be able to accept that God, the Father, can relate directly to us through His Word in a human form in the person of the Messiah. Have you ever asked yourself the question, "If you decided to communicate with a bird and you were able to do anything you wanted, what would be the best way for you to communicate?" The answer is obvious: you would become a bird! Let me illustrate through a story.

The Vietnam war caused a family to be separated. The father was forced to stay in Vietnam, while the wife and two boys were able to come to the United

States. For seventeen years, they communicated with each other only through letters and pictures. The father could see his boys grow up only from a distance.

Then finally the governments of Vietnam and the United States made an agreement that allowed the father to come to the U.S. to see his family. But what if the father said to his family, "I don't really see any need to come see you in person. Communicating through letters and pictures has been sufficient for seventeen years, so it will continue to be sufficient for me." What would you think of such a father? What would you think of a God who, if it were at all possible, would refuse to communicate with His creation in person?[53]

Yes, my dear Muslim reader, certainly Almighty God is able to appear in the person of the Messiah without lessening His essence or staining His divine character. According to the Gospel, Jesus' life on earth was a perfect demonstration of God's love, forgiveness, holiness, healing, purity and salvation.

Jesus Christ, who is described in the Qur'an, Surah 4:171, as God's Word and a Spirit from God, did not lose His divine nature when he was united to human nature. According to the Qur'an and the Gospel, He raised the dead, healed the leper and the blind, and had the ability to create a living being. He had many other unique characteristics which you will discover in the coming chapters that cannot be attributed to a mere man (human being).

Consider the sun, my friend. It sends its rays and penetrates everything that exists on earth. It makes life possible. This occurs without changing the sun's composition. The sun influences the earth and all living beings without it being affected. Can the Creator of that sun, the earth, the human body and all the universe, penetrate our world and be present Himself to save us and accomplish His will without being impaired in any way? Of course He can! "Jesus replied, 'What is impossible with men is possible with God' " (Luke 18:27).

Other Muslims ask, If Christ is God, how was it possible for Him to be killed? Can God die? The Gospel informs us that in the unity of the Godhead there are three persons. One of these is the Son or the Word, who assumed the perfect nature of a man (John 1:14). In His human nature He was hungry, tempted, and crucified. God cannot die but man can. The Gospel contains many statements to show us that Jesus' body was a real human body. In this body He suffered mental anguish and physical pain for our sake. These statements indicate His humanity.

The Gospel also includes many statements indicating His deity. Examples are:

- Eternal: He existed from all eternity (John 8:58 and John 17:5).

- Omnipresent: He is everywhere present at the same time (Matthew 18:20).

- Omniscient: He demonstrated knowledge of things that could only be known if He were God (Luke 6:8; John 4:29).

• Omnipotence: He demonstrated unlimited power
  and authority (Matthew 8:23-27; Matthew 28:18;
  Mark 5:11-15).

Indeed, Jesus had the attributes of a man, but he
also had the attributes of God. Both natures in union
were required to make his atoning work perfect and
our salvation possible.

Some people ask, "How is it possible for the Divine
nature to be united with the human nature?" The
response can be, Whatever the Almighty God decides
to do according to His infinite wisdom, He is also able
to accomplish. The Gospel informs us that the relationship between the humanity of Christ and His
divine nature is such that the humanity is neither
changed into deity nor is the deity lost to His humanity.

It is true that this peculiar relationship is incomprehensible to our limited human intellect. Also many
other things we don't fully understand such as, "How
is it possible for spirit and flesh to be united in man?"
God's Word teaches us clearly that this union of the
Divine and the human nature took place in Christ for
the purpose of satisfying God's justice, manifesting His
love for us and accomplishing our salvation.

My dear Muslim friend, God chose to save us and
elevate us. This was accomplished not only by issuing
an external Divine command but by appearing Himself
in the form of a perfect man to be our personal Savior.
God did not become incarnate in a plant, bird or animal because they do not bear His image. We know from
the Torah, Genesis 1:26, that God created us in His

image. "Then God said, 'Let us make man in our image...' " The Qur'an in Surah 15:29 states: "When I have fashioned him and breathed into him of My Spirit..."

Christian scholar, Kateregga, wrote: "Man created in the image of God does not mean that God looks like man or that man looks like God. But it does mean that man has profound God-like qualities."[54] God created man with the ability to be loving, to be just and compassionate, etc. It is interesting that all of us are aware that we should do better and that we can be better humans. Kateregga continued: "This is the witness of our God — likeness within our conscience. It is a persistent voice in the conscience that we should become better people, that we do not always do what we know we should do, that we really should be more kind, true, reliable, pure, more God-like."[55]

John Gilchrist, lawyer and theologian, writes: "Man was so made that he could possess and manifest all God's characteristic attributes: holiness, love, purity, etc... The question is not whether God can be confined in human form, it is purely whether humanity can bear the divine image. The answer is an unqualified yes. Jesus Christ manifested every one of God's perfect attributes to the full when he lived on earth as a man. There is no reason why the Son of God could not become the Son of Man. In no way was his Divine character blurred while he walked among us. On the contrary God's love, grace, forgiveness and compassion were all revealed to the full when He laid down his life to redeem us from all iniquity and prepare us for a heavenly dwelling."[56]

Jesus — The Perfect Mediator

Jesus, the Messiah, is the perfect Mediator between God and man. In Him we see all the necessary characteristics that must be found in the Mediator "Savior." Only Christ can be called the perfect and acceptable sacrifice to God.

Jesus was human:

It was necessary that the Savior be born under the same law which was broken by every living person. Since man is the one who sinned, it follows that the one who paid the penalty had to be the same as man. It was essential that a human being take our place, suffer and die as a sacrifice on our behalf to pay the penalty for all of our sins. As a man, Christ could represent fallen humanity. And we read in the Bible that Jesus "...shared in their humanity" (Hebrews 2:14).

Jesus understands our struggles because he faced them as a human being. Jesus understands our needs. We read in the Bible, "Because he himself suffered when he was tempted, he is able to help those who are being tempted" (Hebrews 2:18).

Jesus mediates between God and us. As humanity's representative, He intercedes for us before God. As God's representative, He brings us God's salvation and assures us of God's love and forgiveness.

Jesus was without sin:

In the Torah (Leviticus), we see clearly that the Law of God required that the sacrifice offered on the altar be without blemish. Only the sinless can be a substitute for the guilty. The Savior from sin could not himself be a sinner. If he were a sinner:

- He would be dying as a penalty for his own sins and certainly not for the sins of others.

- He would not have enjoyed a distinguished and special relationship with God.

- He could not be the Source of righteousness and eternal life to his followers.

The Messiah was God in the flesh.

To take away the sins of the world the Savior had to pay the full price. Who but a wholly righteous one could satisfy the demand of God's justice? The sacrifice must be of a value equivalent to the number of souls to be redeemed. Nothing but the blood of God's Perfect Lamb is sufficient to wash away all the sins of mankind committed against God. God sent perfection personified. Christ died so that we would have eternal life. Only God in the flesh could defeat Satan and set free those whom Satan held captive.

The Sacrifice Had to Have a Special Relationship to God.

We read about this mystery in the Bible in Colossians 2:9, "For in Christ all the fullness of the Deity lives in bodily form." Jesus alone qualifies as the connecting link between God and man. None but Jesus Christ can give spiritual life to all those who believe in Him because Jesus Christ is alive today in heaven.

CHAPTER 16
THE INCARNATION OF JESUS

In a prophecy concerning the Messiah, Isaiah foretold the union of Deity and humanity in Christ. We read in Isaiah 9:6: "For to us a child is born, to us a son is given, and the government will be on his shoulders. And he will be called Wonderful Counselor, Mighty God, Everlasting Father, Prince of Peace." A child would be born (a reference to His humanity) who would also be the Mighty God (a reference to His Deity).

In the Gospel according to Luke we read that the angel Gabriel (Jibraile) appeared to the virgin Mary and spoke these words: "...'Do not be afraid, Mary, you have found favor with God. You will be with child and give birth to a son, and you are to give him the name Jesus. He will be great and will be called the Son of the Most High...' " (Luke 1:30-32).

Philippians 2:5-11 reads: "Your attitude should be the same as that of Christ Jesus: Who, being in very nature God, did not consider equality with God something to be grasped, but made himself nothing, taking the very nature of a servant, being made in human likeness. And being found in appearance as a man, he humbled himself and became obedient to death — even death on a cross! Therefore God exalted him to the highest place and gave him the name that is above every name, that at the name of Jesus every knee should bow, in heaven and on earth and under the earth, and every tongue confess that Jesus Christ is Lord, to the glory of God the Father."

This passage encourages us to have humility of mind following the example of Christ, who left glory and voluntarily assumed a human body and lived as a servant. The phrase, "...being in very nature God..." particularly refers to Christ's divine nature. This passage continues by saying, "...but made himself nothing, taking the very nature of a servant, being made in human likeness. And being found in appearance as a man, he humbled himself and became obedient to death— even death on a cross!" So this passage shows us that Christ voluntarily emptied Himself. As a man, Christ's glory was veiled to most of the people. We can see in Christ a perfect example of God's own humble Spirit.

In the previously mentioned passage, Christ was made "in human likeness." We understand from the word "likeness" two things: first, that Christ was really like man, and second, that Christ was different from man. He was not identical to man. Christ, by taking on an additional nature (a human nature) and appearing in our world as a man, he relinquished His pre-incarnate position and glory. In His humility and love for us by becoming a man, He subjected Himself voluntarily to many of our human limitations, so He could truly be human like us.

As our representative, He submitted to the Father's will and voluntarily set aside some of His supernatural attributes. Yet, Christ never gave up or surrendered His divine nature. Christ had two natures, one divine and one human. Jesus used His divine power only according to the will of the Father. He did not use these supernatural powers to alleviate

His human suffering or for any personal gain (Matthew 8:20).

THE PURPOSE OF HIS INCARNATION

The reasons for the manifestation of Christ as a man include the following:

- He revealed God the Father to us (2 Corinthians 4:6).

- He provided an example for our lives. Jesus lived as a perfect man. His earthly life showed us the perfect way to live in total and absolute submission to God's will. He also demonstrated how we must serve our fellow man by teaching us to love our neighbor as we love ourselves and even to love our enemies.

Jesus taught us to serve one another. He washed and dried the feet of his disciples. He then said to them: "I have set you an example that you should do as I have done for you" (John 13:15).

He provided an acceptable sacrifice for our sins (Hebrews 10:1-10).

He came to destroy the work of Satan (Shaitan) (1 John 3:8).

The incarnation opened our eyes to the value God places on human life. It assures us of the powerful, deep love that God has for you and me. This is true even in our sinful and fallen states.

JESUS IS BOTH GOD AND MAN

Man attempts to save himself. Man knows that he is the one who has sinned and tries to right the wrong he has done against God. However, man's debt is so great that he could never pay it. Only God could satisfy His own demand for the payment of our sin.

As stated earlier, only one who was both God and man could achieve our salvation. The justice of God requires that man pay the price for his sin. The price that man pays results in separation from God because a sinful man cannot stand before God who is holy. But the love of God extends grace to sinful man through the only vessel that God can use, His Son Jesus Christ. Salvation is accomplished and given by God, for no mere man has the power or the right to earn it. Yet justice requires that someone must pay the penalty for the trespass. Because Jesus was a man, he was able (qualified) to assume our position. Jesus in the form of man took the entire burden of sin upon Himself. He fulfilled the requirement of the law by dying as a man (shedding His blood) for all sins against the Heavenly Father. For this reason the Savior had to be both man and God. Christ was both divine and human. Christ fulfilled the will of God on our behalf. We see in Christ the judgment and the mercy of God in relation to our own sins. We see God as both the Just and the Justifier. Christ is the perfect gift from God to man.

In Christ, God was satisfying his justice. God is just. The Judge of all the earth must do right. Sin is a violation of the Holy Law of God. This is God's moral order. Therefore, it is impossible for God to deal lightly with sin. If our sins could be forgiven at all it must be on a basis which would satisfy the perfect standard of the holiness and justice of God.

To emphasize, we sinners were incapable of eradicating this debt. The Holiness and the justice of God demanded impossible payment. God Himself paid the debt and offered the ultimate sacrifice. He did this because of His perfect love for you and me. On the cross, the price was paid by God. Jesus Christ bore our sins. The Divine Son took man's nature upon Himself. He gave His life for sinners. Christ is the substitute who bears the punishment for us (see 1 Peter 2:24). Through Christ's death, the righteous demands of God's justice have been met.

He suffered not only excruciating physical pain but the spiritual agony of separation from God the Father. Christ bore our sins in His body at the cross. In His incarnation, we can see God identifying Himself with man. The Father did not refrain from the ultimate sacrifice, the life of His Son Jesus, who endured death on the cross so that we might be saved from eternal death and separation from God.

Obedience to the Law can never bring salvation. The law merely shows the sinner that he is guilty before God. The Law demands perfect obedience. Man is not capable of perfection because sin has made us fallible. Under the Law we are condemned. The Good News is: "But when the time had fully come, God sent his Son, born of a woman, born under law, to redeem those under law, that we might receive the full rights of sons" (Galatians 4:4-5).

Before I share more of the Good News with you, my dear reader, I have a request. Please ask God to guide you to His truth and understanding of His Word. This can lead you to a wonderful relationship with Him forever!

SECTION SIX

THE UNIQUE FEATURES OF JESUS

CHAPTER 17
THE VIRGIN BIRTH OF JESUS CHRIST

As we investigate the true uniqueness of Jesus Christ through the Qur'an and the Bible, let us do this with the confidence that God guides us as sincere seekers.

THE VIRGIN BIRTH ACCORDING TO THE QUR'AN AND THE BIBLE

We read in Surah 19:16-34: "Relate in the Book (the story of) Mary, when she withdrew from her family to a place in the east. She placed a screen (to screen herself) from them; Then, We sent to her our angel [Ruhana] and he appeared before her as a man in all respects. She said: 'I seek refuge from thee to (Allah) Most Gracious: (come not near) if thou doest fear Allah.' He said, 'Nay, I am only a messenger from thy Lord, (to announce) to thee the gift of a holy son.' She said: 'How shall I have a son, seeing that no man has touched me, and I am not unchaste?' He said: 'So (it will be)': Thy Lord saith, 'that is easy for Me: and (We wish) to appoint him as a Sign unto men and a Mercy from Us: It is a matter (so) decreed.' So she conceived him, and she retired with him to a remote place..."

Again, the word "our angel" used in this passage is an incorrect translation of the Arabic Qur'anic word, "Ruhana," which means simply "our spirit." Pickthall's translation of the verse is accurate. The Qur'an teaches that Jesus was conceived of a woman only, His Mother - the Virgin Mary. Also, it is important to mention here that the word "announce" used in this passage is an incorrect translation of the Arabic Qur'aic word "Aheb," which means simply "bestow." The virgin birth of Jesus is also recorded in Surah 3:45-47. It is an amazing fact that Jesus' Miraculous Conception is taught in the Qur'an. Surah 21:91 states, "And (remember) her who guarded her chastity. We breathed into her of Our Spirit and we made her and her son a Sign for all peoples."

The Gospel teaches that Jesus was not conceived by human means but by the power of the Holy Spirit of God. We see this clearly in Luke 1:26-36 and Matthew 1:18-21. Both the Bible and the Qur'an teach as a fact that Jesus was born of a virgin woman by the will of God through the power of the Holy Spirit. Jesus was the only man in all creation who was born in this unique way. It is remarkable that the Qur'an states twice that Christ's supernatural birth took place through God's purpose to give men a Sign. Surah 21:91 states, "...and We made her and her son a Sign for all people." In Surah 19:21 we read, "...and (We wish) to appoint him as a Sign unto men and a Mercy from us..." This is not said of any other prophet's birth.

It is also very significant to find that Jesus' mother is the only woman mentioned by name in the entire Qur'an. Surah 19 is named "Maryam (Mary)." It is meaningful to read her name many times in the Qur'an while Eve, the first woman God created, is not mentioned by name. The Qur'an and the Bible teach that Mary is the most honorable woman in the history of mankind. We read in Surah 3:42: "Behold! The angels said: 'O Mary! Allah hath chosen thee and puri-fied thee, chosen thee above the women of all nations.' " In another translation of the Qur'an which is closer to the original Arabic, the same verse says, "And when the angels said: 'O Mary! Lo! Allah hath chosen thee and made thee pure and hath preferred thee above all the women of creation." Read also Luke 1:42.

One must wonder why God chose Mary and honored her above all. The reason is easy and clear — because she was the mother of the most perfect, special and unique man who ever lived on the face of the earth!

Muhammad said: "Satan touches every son of Adam on the day when his mother gives birth to him with the exception of Mary and her son."[57] One should wonder why Jesus' birth was the only birth in which Satan could not interfere. My dear Muslim friend, do you see the uniqueness of Jesus?

THE REASON FOR THE VIRGIN BIRTH ACCORDING TO THE BIBLE

Because Jesus is the Son of God, He must have existed throughout all eternity. Therefore, if the eternal Son of God came in the likeness of a man, He could not have been born of a human father. The life of the human race is passed on by the male seed. Because Jesus is the Son of God, He could not have been procreated by means of a human father. It was absolutely necessary that Jesus be born of a virgin by the power of the Holy Spirit.

Jesus' birth was the only exception to the process of procreation. In fact when Jesus came to this world it was an entry, not a creation. All other men came through the union of a man to a woman. Jesus was conceived entirely by the Spirit of God. The fact that Jesus had this unique beginning to His life on earth demonstrates that He is unique. This is what the angel told Mary when he came to explain Jesus' miraculous conception: "'He will be great and will be called the Son of the Most High'...'The Holy Spirit will come upon you, and the power of the Most High will overshadow you. So the holy one to be born will be called the Son of God'" (Luke 1:32-35).

Jesus' spiritual sonship to the Father explains the necessity of the virgin birth and gives the reason for it. Please read also the following chapter entitled, "Jesus is the Eternal Son of God in a unique spiritual sense."

CHAPTER 18

THE SINLESSNESS OF JESUS CHRIST

No man or prophet has dared to claim infallibility for himself. Only Jesus Christ had complete confidence in His perfection and purity. Therefore, He could boldly ask, "Can any of you prove me guilty of sin? If I am telling the truth, why don't you believe me?" (John 8:46).

THE SINLESSNESS OF JESUS AS DEMONSTRATED IN THE QUR'AN

It is clear from the Qur'an, the Hadith and the Bible that Jesus was the only man who lived without committing a single sin throughout his life. In the Qur'an, Surah 19:19, we read that the angel appeared to Mary and said, "I am only a messenger of thy Lord to announce to thee a gift of a holy son." In another translation of the same Surah 19:19, Jesus is described as being "most pure" (Zakeyia). AL-Baidawi described the Qur'anic phrase, "a boy most pure..." as "pure from sins." Note: in Yusuf Ali's translation of the Qur'an, Jesus is referred to as "holy," in Arberry's translation he is referred to as "pure," and in Pickthall's translation Jesus is referred to as "faultless."

To the Muslim Sufis, Jesus is the example of ultimate purity. The true Sufi longs to be pure like Jesus. Let us read the words of the poet Attar, "Cleanse me, O Lord, of this filthy soul so I may claim immortal purity for myself like Jesus."[58] In the Hadith, Jesus' sinlessness is very clear. Muhammad said: "When any human being is born, Satan touches him at both sides of the body with his two fingers except Jesus, the son of Mary, whom Satan tried to touch but failed."[59] AL-Baidawi explained the meaning of "Satan touches or thrusts" as "to try to entice every newborn so that he can influence the child."[60]

Muhammad also said: "Satan touches every son of Adam on the day when his mother gives birth to him with the exception of Mary and her son."[61] Muhammad said to Ayisha (one of his wives) that every child who is born of Adam's seed is at his birth pricked by Satan, except Jesus and his mother.[62] Suyuti in his writings often quotes Ibn Abbas, from whom Muhammad prompted his adherents to learn the Qur'an. Ibn Abbas was the most knowledgeable person among the people as to what Allah had revealed to Muhammad. Suyuti quotes Ibn Abbas as stating: "Amongst those who were born, only Jesus, son of Mary, was untouched by Satan and not overpowered by him."[63]

In the Gospel Jesus' sinlessness is also very clear, in that:

- "He committed no sin, and no deceit was found in his mouth" (1 Peter 2:22).

- "God made him (Jesus) who had no sin to be sin for us, so that in him we might become the righteousness of God" (2 Corinthians 5:21).

- Jesus Christ is the only person described as sinless in the Qur'an, the Bible, and the Hadith.

ALL HAVE SINNED

It is an easy matter to prove from the Bible, the Hadith and the Qur'an, that all of us have sinned. It is obvious that sin has victory over every human being.

In the Gospel: According to Romans 3:10-12, "There is no one righteous, not even one..."

In the Hadith: The sinfulness of all human beings is confirmed by the well-known Hadith that says, "Satan circulates in the human mind as blood circulates in it."[64]

In the Qur'an: We read in Surah 12:53, "...The (human) soul is certainly prone to evil..." The Qur'an attributes sin to the following prophets:

Adam

"So by deceit he brought about their fall...and their Lord called unto them: "Did I not forbid you that tree...They said: "Our Lord! We have wronged our own souls..." (Surah 7:22-23).

Abraham

"And who, I hope, will forgive me my faults on the Day of Judgment" (Surah 26:82).

Jonah

"Then the big fish did swallow him, and he had done acts worthy of blame" (Surah 37:142).

Moses

"He prayed: 'O my Lord! I have indeed wronged my soul! Do thou then forgive me!" (Surah 28:16).

Muhammad

"that Allah may forgive thee thy faults of the past and those to follow..." (Surah 48:2).

"... and ask forgiveness for thy fault, and for the men and women who believe..." (Surah 47:19).

"...And ask forgiveness for thy fault..." (Surah 40:55).

We also read in the Hadith that Muhammad asked forgiveness and turned to Allah in repentance more than seventy times a day.[65] In the major works of Hadith there are samples of how Muhammad asked for forgiveness. AL-Bukhari recorded the following prayer by Muhammad, "O, Allah! Forgive my mistakes and my ignorance and my exceeding the limits (boundaries) of righteousness in my deeds, and forgive whatever you know better than I. O Allah! Forgive the wrong I have done jokingly or seriously, and forgive my accidental and intentional errors, all that is present in me."[66] Indeed he continued to ask forgiveness until the last breath.[67]

A very well-known Hadith recorded by AL-Bukhari informs us that people were going to the different prophets for intercession, and to all of them the Hadith ascribes sins except Jesus.[68] Ayoub Mahmoud M, a noted contemporary Muslim writer stated, "Jesus is therefore free from the taint of evil and impurity...this purity, which Adam had until he was touched by Satan's finger and thus lost it, now remains exemplified in Jesus alone."[69]

God would certainly be most pleased with one who is truly righteous. "...Verily the most honored of you in the sight of Allah is (he who is) the most Righteous of you..." (Surah 49:13). That *One* is Jesus!

THE GOSPEL GIVES US THE REASON FOR THE SINLESSNESS OF JESUS

In John 10:30 Jesus said, "I and the Father are one." Jesus and the Father are not the same person but they are One in essence and nature. Since the Father and Son are one, as Jesus said, the Son must always do the will of His Father. In John 5:19 Jesus said: "...whatever the Father does the Son also does." Since God the Father can never sin, it follows that Jesus also cannot sin.

Because Jesus is one with God, He always did the absolute will of God. He never did anything independently on His own accord. For this reason He never committed a single sin against God or against another human being. Jesus said in John 8:29: "...for I always do what pleases him."

To be sinless throughout His life, Christ first must have been sinless in His nature. Christ did not have the sin nature that is passed on from Adam to his descendants. He was not conceived through the natural joining of man and woman but through the Holy Spirit. We can see now why Jesus is the only man in human history who lived a sinless life because He is the Son of God.

JESUS CLEANSES US FROM OUR SIN

Read these significant words by Al-Baidawi: "For by His Words religion lives, the human soul lives eternally, and people are cleansed from sin."[70] Jesus is not

only sinless, but also cleanses others from their sins.[71]
We read in the Bible, "If we confess our sins, He is
faithful and just and will forgive us our sins and purify us from all unrighteousness" (1 John 1:9). Please
read also Mark 2:1–12.

Muslims believe that they should be ritually pure
and clean. Muslims wash with clean water before they
pray. If they can't find clean water, then they can use
sand and if sand is not available the person can "reach
out" and touch a clean object to establish the intent
that he be purified. My dear friend, clean water can
clean only our physical body, but you must "reach out"
in a spiritual sense and believe upon the only pure person — Jesus. At the moment you place your trust in
Him, His purity will be applied to you and you will be
worthy to stand and kneel before God.

CHAPTER 19

Unique Features of Jesus' Life

Jesus' Ability to Raise the Dead as Documented in the Qur'an and the Bible

The Qur'an states in explicit language that Jesus actually raised people from the dead. Jesus was quoted in Surah 3:49 as stating, "...And I quicken the dead, by Allah's leave...; surely therein is a Sign for you If ye did believe." Surah 5:110 states that God Himself speaks of Jesus' power to raise the dead. According to the Qur'an, this power has been given only to Jesus. All Muslim commentators on the Qur'an agree that the power to raise the dead belongs only to God. "...He says, 'who can give life to (dry) bones and decomposed ones (at that)?' Say, 'He will give them life who created them for the first time!...'" (Surah 36:78-79).

The Gospel clearly teaches that Jesus had the ability to raise the dead:

> "For just as the Father raises the dead and gives them life, even so the Son gives life to whom he is pleased to give it" (John 5:21).

> "And this is the will of him who sent me, that I shall lose none of all that he has given me, but raise them up at the last day" (John 6:39).

> "No one can come to me unless the Father who sent me draws him, and I will raise him up at the last day" (John 6:44).

When Jesus' friend, Lazarus, died, Jesus told Lazarus' sister, Martha: "...'I am the resurrection and

147

the life. He who believes in me will live, even though he dies; and whoever lives and believes in me will never die...' " (John 11:25-26). Jesus raised Lazarus from the dead to demonstrate that He came to conquer death and give eternal life to whoever believes in Him. Jesus raised Lazarus to prove to us that He possessed absolute power over life and death.

We thank God for what the Bible teaches but realize that we are saved by the Redeemer, Jesus Christ, and not by a doctrine written in a book. My dear Muslim friend, if you are sick, you need a doctor and not a medical book. If you are being sued, you need a lawyer and not a law book. Likewise, when you face your last enemy, death, you need the Savior. Jesus through His resurrection from His tomb, conquered the power of death. He provided the way for whoever would believe in Him to follow Him beyond the grave into Paradise.

JESUS' ABILITY TO CREATE ACCORDING TO THE QUR'AN

According to the Qur'an (Surah 3:49), Jesus was the only man who ever lived who had the power to create a living thing. The Qur'an quoted Jesus: "...I have come to you with a Sign from your Lord, In that I make for you out of clay, as it were the figure of a bird, and breathe into it, and it becomes a bird by Allah's leave..." Surah 5:110 confirms this fact. Jesus created living beings (birds) out of clay the same way that God created Adam. The Qur'an states that only God has the ability to create.

JESUS' ABILITY TO KNOW THE UNSEEN
ACCORDING TO THE QUR'AN AND THE BIBLE

The knowledge of the "unseen" (that which is not seen by human eyes) is a divine quality as the Qur'an states, "With Him are the keys of the unseen, the treasures that none knoweth but He..." (Surah 6:59). Muhammad himself declared in the Qur'an that he did not possess the knowledge of the unseen when he said in Surah 7:188, "If I had knowledge of the unseen, I should have multiplied all good, and no evil should have touched me..." (See also Surah 6:50 and Surah 11:31.)

According to the Qur'an (Surah 3:49), God granted the ability to know the unseen only to Jesus. God chose Jesus out of all His prophets and gave Him the ability to know even the small details of people's lives, including what things they eat and what they treasure up in their houses. Jesus knows the thoughts and the intentions of man as discussed in John 2:24-25, "But Jesus would not entrust himself to them, for he knew all men. For he knew what was in a man." We also learn from the Gospel that Jesus as a prophet predicted specific future events. The following are examples of things that came true:

• His death and resurrection (Matthew 16:21).

• The fall of Jerusalem (Luke 19:43-44).

SOME OTHER UNIQUE FEATURES OF
JESUS' LIFE IN THE QUR'AN

Jesus Is Like Gabriel And Is Like the Holy Spirit:

According to the Muslim scholars, Gabriel is the one used by God to deliver His Word to Muhammad. When AL-Baidawi commented on Surah 5:110 on the confirming of Jesus with the Holy Spirit, he said: "...by 'the Holy Spirit' meaning Gabriel or the Spirit of Jesus."[72] AL-Baidawi, by placing the Holy Spirit alongside the Spirit of Jesus, did not show any distinction between them.

Jesus Is Like the Name of God:

When commenting on Surah 2:87, AL-Baidawi said, "By 'the Holy Spirit' meaning Gabriel, or the spirit of Jesus...or the Majestic Name which Jesus used to raise the dead."

Jesus Is the Only Person in the Qur'an Who Is Called Blessed:

Surah 19:31 says, "And He hath made me Blessed wheresoever I be..." Jesus was blessed *unconditionally* and *continuously*. The word "Blessed," explains AL-Baidawi, means "possessing much profit for others."

Jesus Was Given Complete Revelation:

The Qur'an reports that Jesus had been taught by God the whole of God's revealed Word. Surah 3:48 states, "And Allah will teach him the Book and Wisdom, the Law and the Gospel."

Jesus Was Confirmed By the Holy Spirit:

Surah 2:87 says, "...We gave Jesus, the Son of Mary, clear (Signs) and strengthened him with the Holy Spirit..." According to the Qur'an and the writing of the Muslim scholars, Jesus was the only person who was continuously accompanied by the Holy Spirit from his conception to his ascension. Jesus has the capacity within Him to enjoy every second of His life, being in total harmony with the companionship of the Holy Spirit.

The Muslim commentators knew that what God said in Surah 5:110 is very significant. It states: "Allah say: 'O Jesus the son of Mary! ... Behold! I strengthened thee with the holy spirit...' " AL-Baidawi said of this expression, "with the Holy Spirit may mean with Gabriel, or the spirit of Jesus, or with the words by which the human soul lives eternally, and cleanses (people) from sins, or the majestic name by which Jesus used to raise the dead."[73]

Jesus Is Near-Stationed to God and Forever Eminent:

Jesus is the only person described as being eminent in this world and in the next. In Surah 3:45 we read, "Behold! The angels said: 'O Mary! Allah giveth thee Glad tidings of a Word from Him: His name will be Christ Jesus, the Son of Mary, held in honor in this world and the hereafter and of (the company of) those nearest to Allah.' " Zamakshari, another well known Muslim scholar, explains the meaning of this verse: "The office of prophet and supremacy over men in this world; and in the next world the office of intercessor and loftiness of rank in Paradise." Many Muslim scholars have said, "Eminence in this world means prophe-

cy and precedence over men and in the next intercession and exaltation of position in Paradise." AL-
Baidawi explained the nature of this eminence and
said, "eminence in this life is prophecy, and in the life
to come is intercession."[74]

We read in the Gospel that Jesus is constantly
interceding for His followers. "But because Jesus lives
forever,...he is able to save completely those who come
to God through him, because he always lives to intercede for them" (Hebrews 7:24-25). We also read in
Romans 8:34, "Who is he that condemns? Christ Jesus,
who died — more than that, who was raised to life —
is at the right hand of God and is also interceding for
us."

SECTION SEVEN

THE CRUCIFIXION AND RESURRECTION
OF JESUS CHRIST

CHAPTER 20

THE CRUCIFIXION OF CHRIST ACCORDING TO ISLAM

Many Muslims teach that God would never allow the Jews to crucify Jesus who is described in the Qur'an as a great prophet. I would like to remind these beloved Muslims of verses from the Qur'an that clearly teach of many messengers of God who were killed:

> "...in that they broke their covenant; that they rejected the Signs of Allah; That they slew the messengers in defiance of right..." (Surah 4:155).

> "...that whenever there comes to you a Messenger with what ye yourselves desire not, ye are puffed up with pride? Some ye called impostors, and others ye slay" (Surah 2:87). (Also see Surah 2:91.)

In the entire Qur'an, there is only one passage that speaks on the issue of the crucifixion. It is Surah 4:157-158, which states: "That they said (in boast), 'We killed Christ Jesus the son of Mary, The Messenger of Allah'- But they killed him not, nor crucified him, but so it was made to appear to them,...For of a surety they killed him not...Nay, Allah raised him up unto Himself..." The first question that we need to answer is: To whom was Muhammad referring when he said, "They killed him not, nor crucified him?" The obvious answer from the context is: The Jews. This verse does not say that Jesus was not killed, or that He was not crucified. It merely states that they (the Jews) did not

157

kill or crucify Him. This is true historically, for although the responsibility was theirs, the Roman soldiers actually put Him on the cross.

But there is another sense in which neither the Romans nor the Jews crucified Jesus. Pilate claimed to have the power of life or death over Jesus. However, Jesus declared that Pilate did only the will of God the Father as he gave Jesus over to be crucified. Jesus answered, "you would have no power over me if it were not given to you from above..." (John 19:11). As a matter of fact, we Christians know and believe, based on the Bible, that God was primarily the cause for Jesus' crucifixion. It is very clear in the Bible that Christ's coming, crucifixion, and His work of salvation were planned by God before the world began. (Please read Isaiah 53:10.)

We read in the Qur'an that God caused Jesus to die, and then raised Him up after His death. "Allah said: 'O Jesus! I will take thee and raise thee to Myself And clear thee (of the falsehoods) of those who blaspheme; I will make those who follow thee superior to those who reject faith to the Day of Resurrection...'" (Surah 3:55). The words "I will take thee," in the original Arabic are "innii mutawaffiika" which can only mean "I will cause you to die." This verse clearly states that God is the one who caused the death of Jesus.

THE SUBSTITUTION THEORY

Generally, the Muslim world believes that Jesus was substituted as He faced arrest and death. God changed the face of someone else making this man look like Jesus so that when the Jews and Romans came to arrest Jesus, they thought this man was Jesus and arrested and crucified him by mistake. Based on Surah 4:157-158 and the Hadith, most of the Muslim world believe that at the very moment of this substitution, God lifted Jesus up bodily into heaven. The Muslim scholars are not in agreement on the identity of the person who died in place of Jesus.

LET US TAKE A LOOK AT THE SUBSTITUTION THEORY

Christian scholar E.E. Elder comments on the words, "but so it was made to appear to them." Elder states that, "there is no mention of a substitute here, or anywhere else in the Qur'an. It seems obvious that it cannot refer to Jesus. It certainly must refer to something else that has been mentioned. Now the phrase could be translated, 'it was made a misunderstanding — a perplexity to them.' In that case the subject understood would refer to His crucifixion. The verse could then be properly translated, 'yet they slew him not, and they crucified him not — but it (his crucifixion) was made a misunderstanding to them.' His crucifixion perplexed them. They saw the event, but failed to appreciate its inner meaning. They even thought that they had power over his life."[75]

No one can reach any certain and factual conclusion based on this brief and ambiguous verse in the Qur'an. One way to interpret Surah 4:157-158 is that the Jews thought that the crucifixion of Jesus would shame Him in the eyes of the world. Their intention was that He would suffer ridicule which would destroy Him in the hearts and eyes of the people. They thought that killing Him would invalidate His mission. However, the Jews were wrong. They failed to accomplish their goal. Through the crucifixion the name and person of Jesus was glorified when Allah raised Him up to be with Him. What the unbelieving Jews used to destroy Jesus, God the Father used to exalt the Christ. The Jews thought they were killing the Messiah when Jesus was crucified. They did not realize that their actions actually fulfilled God's plan. God won the victory at the cross by raising Jesus from the dead.

A CLOSER LOOK AT THE SUBSTITUTION THEORY

Not only is the Qur'an's teaching about the crucifixion brief and vague, but the substitution theory itself cannot be believed on moral grounds:

> What kind of God would take an innocent bystander and change his appearance to look like Jesus so that he would be subject to arrest then crucifixion in place of Jesus?

> Why should anyone who was innocent of any capital crime suffer crucifixion? If it were God's desire to rescue Jesus from the hands of the Jews, He could have rescued him without victimizing an innocent person. God did not have to give someone else to the Jews to crucify. That isn't consistent with what we know about the character of a loving, just and merciful God.

The substitution theory portrays God as guilty of misrepresenting one man as another, which is misleading and dishonest. We know that God does not lie.

Some Muslims believe that this was God's way of saving Jesus. If God desired to rescue Jesus through a miracle (perhaps an angelic intercession), He would have done it in a clear manner to prove to the Jews His power and their inability to harm His messenger.

According to the Qur'an, Jesus could have saved Himself because He had the ability to know the unseen. Jesus had the power to raise the dead. He was capable of incredible miracles and dwelt in the continuous company of the Holy Spirit.

The Gospel records the words of Jesus while on the cross. All of them make clear that the person on the cross could only be Jesus. One example is Jesus' statement as recorded in Luke 23:34: "Father, forgive them, for they do not know what they are doing." Can you imagine an innocent victim forced into this agonizing form of execution having an attitude of forgiveness toward those who were crucifying him?

What kind of God would allow Mary, the mother of Jesus, and His beloved friends to suffer in this way? They stood at the cross watching the agony of the one whom they knew to be Jesus (John 19:25-27). Would God allow Jesus' mother to go through this torturous experience because of an illusion that He himself orchestrated?

From what we know about the character of Christ he would never permit another man, even Judas, to suffer the consequences of his own teachings and mission. The cross!

What about the eyewitness testimony of His disciples and followers who saw the crucifixion? Considering what they saw, they believed Jesus was crucified. Was that an inaccurate conclusion? Is it plausible to accept that God would allow the foundation of the Christian faith to be based on an erroneous perception of reality which God Himself fabricated? Such a theory would infer that God lies! Most of Jesus' disciples sacrificed their lives and died a martyr's death because they proclaimed that Christ died on a cross. Did they give their lives for nothing?

Millions of people throughout history have followed these teachings. More than one billion persons today all over the world base their faith on the crucifixion and the resurrection of Jesus! Would God mislead all these people? If so, God is the best liar of all! God forbid!

The substitution theory that the Qur'an advocates, the Hadith teaches, and most of the Muslim world believes, makes God the author of the biggest hoax in human history. This cannot be, God cannot lie. He is a just and Holy God who does only what is right!

I ask you to recognize, my friend, that *Islam does not deny the crucifixion as people usually think.* According to the teachings of the Muslim scholars:

Islam accepts that the Jews plotted to crucify Jesus.

Islam accepts that Jesus was present and that the Jews were seeking to arrest him that Good Friday.

Islam accepts that the man arrested appeared to the Jews to look exactly like Jesus. The Muslim scholars believe that this man who died on the Cross looked exactly like Jesus.

The only thing Islam denies is that the person on the cross was actually Jesus!

MUSLIM SCHOLARS ARE NOT IN AGREEMENT AS TO WHAT HAPPENED TO JESUS

In view of Surah 4:157-158, and other verses in the Qur'an, most of the Muslim scholars believe that Jesus did not die, but that God lifted Jesus up bodily into heaven and He went up alive to heaven. That is how His life on earth ended.

Other well-regarded Muslim scholars do not agree with the majority of the Muslim teachers. Their reasoning is that other Surahs in the Qur'an record Jesus' natural death. One such passage is Surah 19:33, which discusses the death of Jesus very clearly. In this passage Jesus spoke from the cradle to his mother and others. He said: "So peace is on me the day I was born, the day that I die, and the day that I shall be raised up to life (again)." The unmistakable meaning of "the day that I die" is *the day that I will die*. This verse shows clearly that Jesus would die before being brought back to life. The Muslim scholars had a problem. The Qur'an frequently refers to the death of Jesus. Other verses of the Qur'an report that He arose into heaven without dying. These two views are contradictory.

Many Muslim scholars in an attempt to reconcile this contradiction teach that Christ will come back to this world, do many great and wonderful things, and then He will die. The main difficulty with this teaching is that the Qur'an does not state that Jesus is yet to die!

Other texts in the Qur'an that discuss the death of Jesus use the past tense (as something that has already happened). In Surah 19:15 we read about Yahya (John the Baptist) the same words that Jesus spoke about Himself in Surah 19:33: "So peace on him The day he was born, the day that he dies, and the day that he will be raised up to life (again)!" It is a recognized fact that Yahya died and was buried. The reference to being "raised to life again" refers to the Day of Resurrection. Abdullah Yusuf Ali commented on this passage: "This is spoken as in the lifetime of Yahya. Peace and Allah's Blessings were on him when he was born; they continue when he is about to die an unjust death at the hands of the tyrant; and they will be especially manifest at the Day of Judgement."[76]

Muslim Scholar Obaray, commented on Surah 19:33 saying, "No Muslim will shift the death of John to the future. All know that John died...since no one can now shift the death of John to the future, therefore no one can now shift the death of Jesus to the future. In fact there is not one single passage throughout the Qur'an showing that Jesus will return to die. The parallel statement with regard to John who died, clearly shows that Jesus also died."[77] Other passages speak of the natural death of Jesus such as Surah 3:55 and Surah 5:117, which states, "...when thou didst take me up..." Other translations of this verse in the Qur'an read "...take me to thyself..." and "...cause me to die..."(tawaffaitani).

Dr. Mahmud Shaltut, the late Rector of Al Azhar University,[78] said, "The expression tawaffaitani is entitled in this verse to bear the meaning of ordinary death...there is no way to interpret 'death' as occurring after his return from heaven...because the verse very clearly limits the connection of Jesus...to his own people of his own day and the connection is not with the people living at the time when he returns..."[79] Many Muslim writers are confused as they struggle with these texts that talk about the death of Jesus.

Abdullah Yusuf Ali commented on Surah 4:157 which states: "...But they killed him not, nor crucified him..." He said: "The end of the life of Jesus on earth is as much involved in mystery as his birth."[80] He continued his comment on Surah 4:158, which states "Nay, Allah raised him up unto himself..." Ali said: "There is difference of opinion as to the exact interpretation of this verse. The words are: The Jews did not kill Jesus, but Allah raised him up to Himself. One school holds that Jesus did not die the usual human death, but still lives in the body in heaven, which is the generally accepted Muslim view. Another holds that he did die but not when he was supposed to be crucified, and that his being 'raised up' unto Allah means that instead of being disgraced as a malefactor, as the Jews intended, he was on the contrary honored by Allah as His Messenger..."[81]

Distinguished and esteemed Muslim scholars and commentators such as Zamakshari, Ibn Abbas and others stated that Christ remained dead for three to seven hours before being raised to heaven. Maududi, a renowned modern Muslim scholar in Pakistan, comments on Surah 4:157: "After this, God who can do any and everything He wills, raised Jesus to Himself and rescued him from crucifixion and the one who was crucified afterwards was somehow or other taken for Christ."[82] Note the vagueness in his statement.

Daryabadi, another noted Pakastani Muslim theologian said, "It was not Jesus who was executed but another, who was miraculously substituted (how and in what way is another question, and is not touched upon in the Qur'an) for him."[83] This represents yet another obscure statement regarding the crucifixion. Great Muslim scholars such as AL Jalalan, AL-Baidawi and Al Zamkhashri have different opinions as to what happened to Jesus.

Because of the conflicting verses in the Qur'an, many Muslim scholars are confused about the end of the life of Jesus on earth. They disagree about whether He died on earth or was raised alive to heaven. The Muslims have no certain facts or evidence to support their beliefs regarding the end of Jesus' life. They don't have definite information regarding the circumstances surrounding the crucifixion.

CHAPTER 21
THE CRUCIFIXION AND RESURRECTION OF JESUS ACCORDING TO THE GOSPEL

The Gospel is consistent within itself about the subject. Christ was crucified, died and rose from the dead. Because of the clear testimony of the Bible to these facts, for nearly two thousand years Christians throughout the world unanimously have believed in the crucifixion, death and resurrection of Jesus Christ. For example the Apostle Peter, speaking to the Jews after healing a man, says, "Then know this, you and all the people of Israel: It is by the name of Jesus Christ of Nazareth, whom you crucified but whom God raised from the dead, that this man stands before you healed" (Acts 4:10).

In John 8:20 and John 17:1, we can see clearly that the crucifixion is spoken of as the important "hour" for which Christ came. It was the mission of Jesus to die on the cross as the final and perfect sacrifice, once and for all! (Also see Hebrews 9:28 and Luke 18:31-34.)

OLD TESTAMENT PROPHECIES REGARDING JESUS' CRUCIFIXION

The Gospel illustrates many details of the crucifixion. The Old Testament prophecies predict and depict the crucifixion hundreds of years before it actually took place. Two of these prophecies are found in Isaiah 53 and Psalm 22.

Jesus' Death and Burial: (Isaiah 53:9)

Isaiah 53:9 gives us specific details about the death of Jesus: "He was assigned a grave with the wicked, and with the rich in his death ..." No one at the time of Isaiah could understand the meaning of this verse. It does not make sense at face value. The account of His burial sounds like a contradiction. Did they bury him with the outcast or bury him with the noble and rich?

Christ was crucified between two thieves and according to Roman law, criminals that were crucified were to be thrown into a burning pit and cremated. However for Jesus, this was not actually done. Both seemingly contradictory statements in Isa 53:9 were reconciled. Jesus' death was with the wicked, between two thieves on the cross,[84] fulfilling the first part of this prophecy. The second half of this prophecy was fulfilled in the Gospel, Matthew 27:57-60: "As evening approached, there came a rich man from Arimathea, named Joseph, who had himself become a disciple of Jesus. Going to Pilate, he asked for Jesus' body, and Pilate ordered that it be given to him. Joseph took the body, wrapped it in a clean linen cloth, and placed it in his own new tomb that he had cut out of the rock." What seems an unexplained paradox in Isaiah 53 is given a very simple explanation in the Gospel according to Matthew.

Dividing of Christ's Clothes: (Psalm 22:18)

In another prophecy about the death of Christ, found in the Psalms of David, is Psalm 22:18. It states: "They divide my garments among them and cast lots for my clothing." This verse also was a mystery and a riddle to the people at that time. It seems like the writer said one thing, then contradicted himself. Did they take the clothes and divide them amongst themselves or did they cast lots to see who would get the garments?

This prophecy was *exactly* fulfilled in John 19:23-24. When the soldiers crucified Jesus, they took his clothes, dividing them into four shares, one for each of them, with the undergarment remaining. This garment was seamless, woven in one piece from top to bottom. In effect, the soldiers said to one another, "Let's not tear it, but decide by lot who will get it." They gambled to see who would win it. This happened that the scripture might be fulfilled which said, "They divide my garments among them and cast lots for my clothing." So this is what the soldiers did. The strange paradoxical statement of Psalm 22:18 was explained and fulfilled to the letter at the foot of the Cross.

Those are two examples of the fine details which the Bible gives us regarding Jesus' crucifixion, hundreds of years before the crucifixion occurred.

Incidentally, note that the Jews who rejected Jesus and did not accept Him as the Son of God or their Savior dared not delete any one of the many prophecies that were fulfilled in Him.

THE CRUCIFIXION IS CERTAINLY A HISTORIC FACT

The crucifixion of Jesus is one of the best-attested events in past history. No educated modern historian doubts that Jesus was a historical character or that he was crucified. One of the most acclaimed Muslim thinkers and writers in the history of Egypt, Abaas Mahmood Al Akad, wrote a book about the life of Christ, in which he confirmed that we can depend on the four

Gospels as historic evidence to know what happened in Jesus' life.[85]

It is not rational to believe the claim, made 600 years after Christ's crucifixion, that the person who was crucified was not Christ but rather a look-a-like substitute. An example would be if a man would come hundreds of years from now and tell the world that the one who was assassinated in the Twentieth Century was not John F. Kennedy but rather someone else who looked exactly like him. Again, the crucifixion of Christ is an historic fact supported by many eyewitnesses.

If the Biblical and historic records of the crucifixion were untrue, it would be reasonable to expect the Qur'an to have many verses clearly stating Jesus did not die on the cross. The amazing truth is that in the 6,000 plus Qur'anic verses, there is not a single verse that simply and clearly states that Jesus was never crucified, showing that Christians were mistaken and that the Gospel is incorrect on this point. *Not one!*

Jesus' crucifixion actually demonstrated what the word "Muslim" means and stands for. The word "Muslim" means one who surrenders and submits. Jesus obeyed God to the end. He submitted his life to the will of God, just as Abraham's son submitted himself and obeyed his father's instructions leading him to the altar to be sacrificed. We as Christians see the crucifixion as giving the greatest honor to Jesus. We also see the power of God in raising Jesus from the dead and accomplishing our salvation.

The Qur'an ignored not only the records of Matthew, Mark, Luke and John but the entire New

Testament. Muslim scholars also disregarded the historical evidence. Non-Christian authors from the time of Christ discussed Jesus and His crucifixion as an historical fact. Consider the non-Christian author, Flavius Josephus, for example.

Flavius Josephus (37 - 100 A.D.):

Joseph ben Matthias was a Jewish historian born of a priestly family, and he descended from the Judaic royal lineage. He became a Pharisee devoted to the study of the Law of God and became a Roman citizen named Flavius Josephus.

Josephus continued to live in the area of Jerusalem. Josephus became the eyes and ears of Judaism to Rome. He then gained access to first hand information. He documented Jewish history and traditions for Rome.[86] With no ties to the Christian sect, there was no reason for him to fabricate or embellish his records. His background validated his writings as important and objective proof of the events in the life of Jesus (i.e. His crucifixion and His resurrection). Regarding Jesus, Josephus wrote:

> "Now, there was about this time, Jesus, a wise man, if it be lawful to call him a man, for he was doer of wonderful works ... a teacher of such men as receive the truth with pleasure. He drew over to him both many of the Jews, and many of the Gentiles. He was [the] Christ; and when Pilate, at the suggestion of the principal men amongst us, had condemned him to the cross, those that loved him at the first did not forsake him, for he appeared to them alive

again the third day, as the divine prophets had foretold these ... and the tribe of Christians, so named from him, are not extinct at this day."[87]

Josephus had first-hand access to individuals (both Christian and non-Christian) who had been eyewitnesses to the events surrounding the life, death and resurrection of Jesus Christ. As a modern historian of his day, the facts reported in his journals were held accountable. These reports were under the scrutiny of diametrically opposed factions. To this day he is considered to be a reputable historian. Josephus documented accounts of individuals who witnessed Jesus' miracles, his teaching, his arrest and trial, and his crucifixion and resurrection.

JESUS CAME BACK FROM THE DEAD

Jesus' disciples believed in His resurrection because they actually saw him alive after His crucifixion and death. The account of Jesus' resurrection is found in the following passage: "The angel said to the women, 'Do not be afraid, for I know that you are looking for Jesus, who was crucified. He is not here; he has risen, just as he said. Come and see the place where he lay. Then go quickly and tell his disciples: He has risen from the dead and is going ahead of you into Galilee. There you will see him. Now I have told you' " (Matthew 28:5-7). They saw the Risen Christ over a forty day period following His resurrection, in a variety of locations and times (Luke 24:34; John 20:26-28; Acts 1:3). Jesus was seen by over 500 brethren at once in his resurrected body (1 Corinthians 15:1-6).

Professor Thomas Arnold, the Lord Master of Rugby University, author of *The History of Rome* and holder of the Chair of Modern History at Oxford University, was well equipped to evaluate evidence to determine historical fact. After carefully sifting the ancient documentation for the crucifixion and resurrection of Christ, the renown scholar wrote: "I have been used for many years to study the histories of other times and to examine and weigh the evidence of those who have written about them. I know of no one fact in the history of mankind which is proven by better and fuller evidence of every sort, to the understanding of a fair inquirer, than the great sign which God has given us that Christ died and rose again from the dead."

John Capeley, a professor at Cambridge University, rose to the highest office as a Judge in England. He was recognized as one of the greatest legal minds in British history. He stated, "I know pretty well what evidence is and I tell you, such evidence as that for the resurrection has never been broken down yet."

Christians and non-Christians agree about three specific historic facts:

• Jesus Christ was crucified.

• There was an empty tomb.

• There was an Easter proclamation that Jesus had Risen.

As previously pointed out, Jesus Christ was crucified. After His death He was taken down from the cross and laid in the tomb of Joseph of Arimathea. Historic documents state that a large stone weighing between one and two tons was placed at the front of the tomb and the Roman seal was placed on that stone. Well-trained Roman guards were watching the tomb. Three days later, the tomb was empty.

Following Jesus' death, His disciples were afraid and they hid (Matthew 26:56). Within several days after the resurrection this same group became courageous. This happened not only because they had seen an empty tomb but because they had seen the risen Christ.

If someone asks, "Did these disciples lie?" the answer is simple. What would they gain by proclaiming that Jesus is risen and that they had seen Him alive? Prestige? Wealth? History tells us that except for one of them, all died a martyr's death. Some examples of their execution include: Jude and Simon were crucified, Luke was hanged from an olive tree, Paul was beheaded, Philip was scourged and crucified, James (son of Zebedde) was killed by the sword. Mark was dragged through the streets by his feet and then burned alive. Barnabus and James (brothers of Jesus) were stoned to death. This was their reward for claiming that Jesus is risen, that He is alive, that He offers forgiveness of sins, and gives eternal life to those who believe in Him.

SECTION EIGHT

THE ASCENSION AND RETURN OF JESUS CHRIST

CHAPTER 22
THE ASCENSION OF JESUS

The Ascension of Jesus is clearly stated in the Qur'an and clearly explained in the Bible.

THE QUR'AN'S ACCOUNT OF THE ASCENSION OF JESUS

It is very clear from many verses in the Qur'an that Jesus was lifted up to be with God and is alive today. For example, Surah 4:158 states: "...Allah raised him unto Himself..." Surah 3:55 recounts: "...Allah said: 'O Jesus! I will take thee and raise thee to Myself...' "

Al Imam Al Razi, a prominent Muslim scholar, comments on Surah 4:158: "the lifting up of Jesus to God as a reward is greater than Paradise and all that is in it of physical pleasures. And that verse opens to you the door of the knowledge of spiritual joys." [88] What could be greater than Paradise and all the physical pleasures which that entails? According to Al Razi the answer is God's Presence.[89] In a different writing Al Razi said that the meaning of "I will raise thee to Me" is actually "I am raising thee to the presence of My honor."[90]

There are many Hadiths supporting the ascension of Jesus. Generally, the Muslim world believes that God lifted Jesus up bodily into heaven and that he went up alive to heaven. The Bible records the Ascension of Jesus (Acts 1:9-11; Acts 7:55-56).

Both the Qur'an and the Bible teach that Jesus ascended not just into heaven but indeed above the heavens into the ultimate presence of God. The Qur'an and the Bible agree on the fact that Jesus Christ is alive in heaven to this day. Contrary to the biblical account, the reason many Muslim scholars give for the ascension of Jesus is that God took him to heaven to save him from the murderous intentions of the Jews.

The reason which the Muslim scholars give is not sufficient to explain the fact that God has enjoyed the presence of Jesus for nearly two thousand years after His death. It is very difficult to accept the theory that "God took Jesus up to Himself" just as an escape route to save him from the hands of the Jews. First of all, God could have used ordinary ways to deliver Jesus. We have an example in the Gospel according to Matthew 2:13. When Herod wanted to kill Jesus, an angel warned Joseph in a dream and told him to take the child and his mother and flee to Egypt.

In addition, Jesus could have saved himself from the hands of the Jews if he had wanted. According to the Qur'an:

• Jesus has the ability to know the unseen (Surah 3:49).

• Jesus has the ability to perform miracles (Surah 5:110).

My dear Muslim friend, the logical conclusion is that it was the desire of God to raise Jesus to be with Him. He did not have to raise Him to save him from the "murderous intentions of the Jews." The Qur'an does not explain why God desired and willed to have Jesus abide with him in heaven in glory for nearly 2,000 years. According to the Qur'an, Jesus was the only human to be raised off the earth into the very presence of God Himself. How could a mere man be lifted up to be with God? How could a mere man stand the majesty, the power and holiness of the Most High?

THE BIBLE REVEALS THE REAL REASON
FOR THE ASCENSION OF JESUS

Jesus is the Son of God and heaven is His home. Therefore, it was impossible for Him after He accomplished His mission on earth to go to the dust like all other prophets and men naturally do. John 6:38 records Jesus saying, "For I have come down from heaven not to do my will but to do the will of Him who sent me." We read also in John 3:13 that Jesus spoke of Himself saying, "No one has ever gone into heaven except the one who came from heaven — the Son of Man." In John 8:23 Jesus told the Jews, "...You are from below; I am from above. You are of this world; I am not of this world."

Remember, my dear Muslim reader, what the Qur'an said in Surah 4:171 about Jesus, that He is a "Spirit proceeding from God." It is obvious then that only He who came from God could go back to be with God. Jesus' ascension to heaven was a necessity because He is the Son of God. Isn't it amazing, my dear reader! Jesus must have the quality of life in Himself that makes Him at home with the Majesty and Holiness of God.

The ascension of Christ meant the end of His earthly ministry and the beginning of His heavenly ministry. It also meant that God accepted Jesus' service and sacrifice on earth. My dear friend, Jesus Christ without a doubt is in reality higher than all. He is alive with the Heavenly Father today!

CHAPTER 23

THE SECOND COMING OF JESUS

ISLAM AND CHRISTIANITY ACKNOWLEDGE THAT JESUS IS COMING BACK

Surah 43:61 states, "And (Jesus) shall be A Sign (for the coming of) the Hour (of judgement)..." Abdullah Yusuf Ali commented on this verse in his translation of the Qur'an and said, "This is understood to refer to the second coming of Jesus in the Last Days before the resurrection when he will destroy the false doctrines that pass under his name..."[91]

Throughout the centuries, most of the Muslim commentators interpret Surah 43:61 as a prophecy of the descent of Jesus to earth. It is interesting my dear Muslim friend, to read about this very same fact in the Old Testament. Daniel 7:13-14 tells us: "In my vision at night I looked, and there before me was one like a son of man, coming with the clouds of heaven. He approached the Ancient of Days and was led into his presence. He was given authority, glory and sovereign power; all peoples, nations and men of every language worshiped him. His dominion is an everlasting dominion that will not pass away, and his kingdom is one that will never be destroyed." This is a clear prophecy of the Second Coming of Jesus Christ that was confirmed in the Gospel of Mark 13:26, which reads, "At that time men will see the Son of Man coming in clouds with great power and glory."

Muslims and Christians teach that Jesus will return from heaven heralding the climax of human history and will assume control over the whole world. Jesus alone is to herald the hour of judgment. Ibn-Atya, a distinguished Muslim commentator, stated that "Muslim theologians are unanimous in contending that Jesus Christ is physically alive at present in heaven and is destined to return to this world... towards the approach of the Last Day."[92]

Of course the Hadith teaches very clearly that Jesus will return from heaven in the last days. There are approximately seventy traditions in support of the doctrine of the return of Jesus to earth. All of them are considered to be of unquestioned reliability. Muhammad said, "Jesus will return to earth to receive the homage of all to whom the Scriptures have been given."[93] Muhammad also said, "The son of Mary (may peace be upon him) will soon descend among you and will judge mankind justly (as a just ruler)."[94] Who is this man who can judge every person justly? Don't you wonder, my friend?

THE BIBLE EXPLAINS WHY JESUS IS COMING BACK

It is natural to believe that the Son of God will be the One chosen to descend from heaven to bring the judgment of God.

The Son of God by coming in the likeness of man has revealed God to men and has brought men face to face with God. "Moreover, the Father judges no one, but has entrusted all judgment to the Son, that all may honor the Son just as they honor the Father. He who does not honor the Son does not honor the Father, who sent him" (John 5:22-23).

Speaking of Jesus, the Bible states: "For as the Father has life in himself, so he has granted the Son to have life in himself. And he has given him authority to judge because he is the Son of Man" (John 5:26-27). (Read also Matthew 24:30.)

When Jesus comes back again He will be shining with all the brightness of His heavenly glory. This biblical teaching makes sense. He has been in heaven for nearly 2,000 years. We read, "When the Son of Man comes in his glory, and all the angels with him, he will sit on his throne in heavenly glory" (Matthew 25:31). Jesus will be the most glorious sight that humans have ever seen. Jesus will come back as a conquering and victorious Lord to put an end to evil and rule with Holy justice!

His return will make all the people who believe in Him just like Himself. At His second coming, He will transform "true Christians" (followers of Jesus) into His image as He comes back to share His glory forever. We read about this glorious fact in the Gospel, "As was the earthly man, so are those who are of the earth; and as is the man from heaven, so also are those who are of heaven. And just as we have born the likeness of the earthly man, so shall we bear the likeness of the man from heaven" (1 Corinthians 15:48-49).

Jesus will give us new, glorified bodies suited for heaven. Jesus' first coming was to make Himself like us - Jesus' second coming is to make us like Him:

"...we know that when he appears, we shall be like him, for we shall see him as he is" (1 John 3:1-3).

"But our citizenship is in heaven. And we eagerly await a Savior from there, the Lord Jesus Christ, who, by the power that enables him to bring everything under his control, will transform our lowly bodies so that they will be like his glorious body" (Philippians 3:20-21).

"For the Lord himself will come down from heaven, with a loud command, with the voice of the archangel and with the trumpet call of God, and the dead in Christ will rise first. After that, we who are still alive and are left will be caught up together with them in the clouds to meet the Lord in the air. And so we will be with the Lord forever. Therefore encourage each other with these words" (1 Thessalonians 4:16-18).

My dear Muslim friend, the purpose of Jesus' coming into our world is to save us and give us eternal life. The Good News of the Bible is that Jesus is returning to our world to gather all of those who believe in Him. He will take them home to be with Him in heaven forever. Jesus told us, "Do not let your hearts be troubled. Trust in God; trust also in me. In my Father's house are many rooms; if it were not so, I would have told you. I am going there to prepare a place for you. And if I go and prepare a place for you, I will come back and take you to be with me that you also may be where I am" (John 14:1-3).

CHRIST IS GOD'S CHOICE FOR THE LAST BATTLE ACCORDING TO ISLAM

According to the Hadith a false Christ, "Dajjal," will appear before the Hour of Doom. The Dajjal (means "the deceiver" in Arabic) will pretend he is the Christ. Christians know this individual as the Antichrist. He will perform many miracles. According to the Hadith, the false Christ will be the ultimate manifestation of evil. He will cause the greatest assault on faith against the only true God. He will attempt to cause the greatest harm to mankind. Muhammad said, "From the creation of Adam until the Hour of Doom there is nothing more dangerous than the false Christ."[95] We read in one of the most authentic and reliable Hadiths that Muhammad frequently prayed, "Oh, God, I take refuge in you from the torment of the grave and the torment of Hell...and the trial of the false Christ."[96]

In following reliable narration in the Hadith, it is recorded that Ayisha (one of Muhammad's wives) said: "I heard Allah's Apostle (Muhammad) in his prayer seeking refuge with Allah from the affliction of AL-Masih Ad-Dajjal."[97] According to the Hadith, Christ, Isa, is the only One whom God will send to defeat the false Christ, save mankind, restore faith in the true God and establish peace on earth.

Suyuti, a very credible Muslim scholar, uses a Hadith in which the false Christ deceives multitudes of people by his miracles. Suyuti said: "the Dajjal will proceed towards Bait al-Maqdes... While the Muslims are preparing their arrows to fight him, the shadow of the false Christ falls on them. Their most powerful men begin to kneel down, others sit down from hunger,

while others faint. At that time they hear a voice crying, 'Your rescue has come to you...' Then the earth will
shine with the light of its Lord and Jesus, Son of Mary,
will descend...Jesus will kill the false Christ...people
will live for forty years. No one will die, no one will get
sick."[98] During the rule of Jesus, death will be inactive
and it will hold no power over man. How amazing is
the power of Jesus! Not only does he have the ability to
raise the dead but also to conquer the power of death.

It is very fascinating that the Hadith states, "Then
the earth will shine with the light of its Lord and
Jesus, Son of Mary, will descend..." For we read about
Jesus in the Gospel, Matthew 17:2: "There he was
transfigured before them. His face shone like the sun,
and his clothes became as white as the light."
According to the Hadith, Jesus will appear from heav-
en in power and glory.

The Hadith proclaims, "Jesus, Son of Mary, will
descend...and will lead them in prayer. When the
enemy of Allah (The Dajjal) sees him, he will dissolve
just as salt dissolves in water..."[99] It is very thought
provoking, my dear reader! Only Jesus, without the
assistance of other prophets or angels, will win the
most important and crucial battle in the history of
humanity. Another Hadith states that during the reign
of Jesus, "Spite, mutual hatred and jealousy against
one another will certainly disappear."[100]

"Then a people whom Allah had protected would
come to Jesus, Son of Mary, and he would wipe their
faces and would inform them of their ranks in
Paradise."[101] How amazing! Who is this man who will
tell people their degrees in Paradise before the day of

judgment? Jesus knows the eternal destiny of all people because He is Divine.

Muhammad said, "I warn you of him and there is no prophet who has not warned his people against the Dajjal..."[102] Isn't it interesting, my dear Muslim reader, that every prophet came to warn his nation of the deception of the Dajjal, but Christ alone will come again to destroy him?

WHAT DOES THE UNIQUENESS OF JESUS IMPLY AND DEMAND?

My dear Muslim friend, I pray that you would continue to ask for God's guidance to the straight path that leads to Him. Be sincere in evaluating and accepting the truth that He reveals to you. These unique features in the life of Jesus prove that He is more than a mere prophet. The prophets we have come to know through the Bible and the Qur'an were ordinary men. They were born of a father and a mother. They lived a normal life. Sometimes they did good things and other times sinned against God and against their fellow human beings. Their lives ended naturally and they returned to the dust from where they came. Thus the prophets' lives were not distinguished from all other men in a supernatural way.

We learn from the Qur'an and the Bible that Jesus' life was unique. He was set apart even before conception. Jesus' virgin birth tells us that God miraculously made an exception to His process of procreation, to have Jesus conceived in the womb of a virgin by the power of God's Spirit. The sinlessness of Jesus, His ability to create, to raise the dead, His Ascension, and

His inevitable return to take control of this world (to herald the Day of Judgment) demand the conclusion that He is more than just a prophet. He is the unique, eternal Son of God!

My dear Muslim brothers and sisters, ask yourself: Why are all these unique, distinguished and heavenly features found only in Jesus Christ? The idea that Jesus Christ was merely a prophet and messenger does not seem reasonable when we consider the many unique features that are found only in Him. This emphasizes His distinguished relationship to God, and His unique character and mission. We should also notice that Jesus' uniqueness is totally the result of the special will and power of God. It was according to the plan of God alone that Jesus had such exceptional life and honor. When you prayerfully ponder Jesus' life, you cannot ignore the evidence that there is something majestic about the man Jesus. There is something particularly glorious and supernatural about the person of Jesus.

All these unique features in Jesus' life find their meaning and significance in the most essential doctrines of Christianity, which are: Jesus is the eternal, unique Son of God, and He alone is the Savior of mankind. And it is through discovering Jesus' uniqueness that we can understand the significance of the Christian faith. Both the Qur'an and the Gospel attribute three titles to Jesus which are consistent with and support the Christian belief in Him as Lord and Savior. These divine titles are: "the Word of God," "the Messiah," and "Spirit from God."

SECTION NINE

THE MYTH OF THE THREE GODS
OF CHRISTIANITY

CHAPTER 24
DO CHRISTIANS WORSHIP THREE GODS?

The Bible clearly reveals that there is only one God. Jesus said, "...The Lord our God, the Lord is one" (Mark 12:29-30). You can read that the Lord Jesus Christ Himself taught this belief. In these verses He quoted the famous passage in the Torah, Deuteronomy 6:4-5, "Hear, O Israel: The LORD our God, the LORD is one. Love the LORD your God with all your heart and with all your soul and with all your strength."

The first commandment given to Moses was, "You shall have no other gods before me" (Exodus 20:3). The apostle James wrote, "You believe that there is one God. Good!..." (James 2:19). Matthew recorded the words of Christ to His disciples: "Therefore go and make disciples of all nations, baptizing them in the name[103] of the Father and of the Son and of the Holy Spirit, and teaching them to obey everything I have commanded you. And surely I am with you always, to the very end of the age" (Matthew 28:19-20). (Read also 1 Corinthians 8:4.)

The Bible also reveals that the nature of God is compound, which means there is plurality in the one-ness of God. In the book of Genesis we read: "Then God said, 'Let us make man in our image, in our likeness, and let them rule over the fish of the sea and the birds of the air, over the livestock, over all the earth, and over all the creatures that move along the ground.' So God created man in His own image, in the image of

God he created him; male and female he created them"
(Genesis 1:26-27). The italics added in this verse draw
attention to the fact that there is a combination of singular and plural tenses in the scriptures, which were
inspired by God Himself.

The universal Christian creed begins, "I believe in
one God." Christians believe in one God and regard
polytheists (those who believe in more than one God)
as unbelievers. The Gospel teaches us that God is one
essence who reveals Himself in three persons. They
are the Father, Son [Jesus, AL-Masih, the Word], and
Holy Spirit. Please read 2 Corinthians 13:14 and
Ephesians 2:18.

The unity of God is the most essential characteristic of the Trinity. It is because of the Christian belief in
the absolute unity of one God, that we recognize
Father, Son and Holy Spirit as divine. God is one. If
this is not true then the Trinity does not exist. Many
Muslims mistakenly think that Christians believe in
three gods: Mary, Jesus and God. On this issue Ibn
Abbas said: "What is meant by the Trinity is God the
most high, His consort and His Son."[104] .They base
their opinion on the Qur'an:

> "Say not 'Trinity' ..." (Surah 4:171). The correct
> translation of the Arabic words in this verse
> are: "And do not say three (Thalathah)..."
> (Surah 4:171). "Three" not "trinity" is the cor-
> rect translation of the Arabic word
> "Thalathah."

> "They do blaspheme who say: Allah is one of
> three (Thalathah)..." (Surah 5:73).

The word "thalathah" appears nineteen times in the Qur'an and is always translated "three." This refers to the simple numerical digit number "three." The Qur'an makes no reference to the Christian belief in the Triune God. Only when Muslim scholars translated the Qur'an to English did they add the word trinity. This word is never found in the original Arabic Qur'anic text.

The Qur'an rejects the belief in three gods. However it identifies the second and third persons as Mary and Jesus. We read in Surah 5:75 that, "Christ, the son of Mary, was no more than a Messenger..., His mother was a woman of truth. They had both to eat their (daily) food..." Clearly the Qur'an intended that they couldn't be God because they needed to eat food to survive. Like everybody else, they were both humans. We know that God does not need any sustenance. The Qur'an gives the impression that the Trinity consists of God, Jesus and Mary. "...Allah will say: 'O Jesus the son of Mary! didst thou say unto men, 'Worship me and my mother as gods in derogation of Allah?' " (Surah 5:116).

The Qur'an denounces a doctrine which taught the existence of three gods. This is not the Christian doctrine of the Holy Trinity. The Holy Trinity is one God. In this Divine Unity there are three eternal Persons of one substance and power. It is clear that the Christian doctrine is quite a different thing. The Qur'an testifies that Christians are monotheistic and are not infidels. The following are examples of this testimony:

Surah 29:46: "And dispute ye not with the people of the Book, except with means better (than mere disputation)...but say, 'We believe in the Revelation which has come down to us and in that which came down to you; our God and your God is One; and it is to Him we bow...' " Thus it is clear that the Qur'an testifies that Christians "people of the Book" worship one God.

Surah 5:82: "Strongest among men in enmity to the believers wilt thou find the Jews and pagans; and nearest among them in love to the believers wilt thou find those who say "We are Christians," because amongst these are men devoted to learning..." Here are presented three groups: Jews, pagans (idolaters), and Christians, of which the Christians are given the highest praise. (See also Surah 2:62 and Surah 3:113-114.)

Note that Islam forbids the Muslim to marry an idolatress, but it does not forbid him to marry a Christian because Christians are people who know God and worship only Him.

It is important to mention here that even though the majority of Roman Catholic, Orthodox, and Protestant churches disagree on many secondary issues, they have never even slightly disagreed or have controversy over the doctrine of the Tri-unity. The reason is simply that the Church did not invent this doctrine, but rather discerned it from an objective study of the Bible.

CHAPTER 25
UNDERSTANDING THE TRI-UNITY OF GOD

There isn't any symbol in the physical universe that can adequately picture the Tri-Unity of God. Christians cannot ultimately explain or define the Trinity in human words. The impossibility of explaining the Tri-Unity of God shows that humans did not invent this doctrine. No one can give an illustration of the Trinity that truly explains the God who created the heavens and the earth. Consider how long it took the world to discover and understand simple facts about the universe, the earth, the human body, etc. We are still very far from knowing everything that relates to our (physical environment) world. It is not surprising that it is impossible for us to explain the God who controls the world. God's nature and essence cannot be completely understood by us, mere humans. We are unable to comprehend infinite God with our finite minds. God's nature lies outside our experience and knowledge. God is transcendent.

The oneness of God in Islam is described in finite terms, but the Christian doctrine of tri-unity is infinite and indescribable. The early church did not invent the doctrine of the Trinity. It just accepted it from what God had revealed about Himself in the Gospel.[105]

Consider that each man is one, but his unity is more complex than that of a one-celled bacteria. If the oneness of man involves spiritual aspects as well as physical, surely the concept of the oneness of God is

not diminished by seeing complexity within that oneness. Since we know that God is infinite, we must
agree that His potential is unlimited. The possibilities
of His complex nature suggests areas that are incon-
ceivable to our earthly mind. If He is a triune God, who
are we to say He cannot be? Father, Son and Holy
Spirit are one in essence, will, nature, power and eter-
nality. This is the doctrine of the Trinity which
Christians believe according to the Gospel.

Many of my Muslim friends think that this doctrine of the Trinity contradicts itself. They say, "How
can something be three and one?" In response,
Christian scholar Dean Halverson explains, "For a
statement to contradict itself it must both affirm and
deny the same thing in the same respect. Does the doctrine of the Trinity do that? The answer is no, because
the doctrine states that God is one essence (or being, or
substance) and three in person. Essence and personhood are different. God is three in person, in that each
person of the Trinity is distinct within the Godhead.
God is one, in that each person of the Godhead shares
the same self-existing essence and other qualities
unique to God. This simultaneous distinction and
sameness is seen in John 1:1."[106]

So the concept is not 1 + 1 + 1 = 3. Rather, it is 1 x
1 x 1 = 1. In John 14:10, Jesus tells Philip, that He is
in the Father and that the Father is in Him. The
Gospel in Matthew 10:20 records that the Holy Spirit
is the Spirit of God. In Galatians 4:6, the Holy Spirit is
called the Spirit of Jesus.

AL-Ghazzali answered a similar question about tri-
unity. As one of the most respected Muslim theologians

in the history of Islam, he is known as the "Martin Luther" of the Muslims. He said, "How can the many be one? Know that this is the goal of all revelations, and the secrets of this science should not be penned down in a book, for the people of knowledge said, the unveiling of the secret of Lordship is blasphemy...the thing can be many in one sense, but also can be one in another sense. And so, as man is many in one sense if you look at his spirit and body and limbs and blood vessels and bones and members, but in another sense, he is one man."[107]

In the Gospel this unity exists, three persons in one essence, indivisible and inseparable. The famous Muslim Imam Shaarani acknowledges, "Convention plurality does not preclude essential unity, such as the branches of a tree in relation to its root or the fingers in relation to the palm."[108]

Christians agree with Muslims that God is one, entirely distinct from all created beings. But we have not yet begun to deal with the issue of what mysteries the Divine Nature may contain in itself. Mysteries are inherent in the supreme divine nature of God. Therefore, whatever our beliefs, whether we hold onto the Muslim's belief about the singular oneness of God's nature or the Christian belief in the compound unity of God's nature, neither conflict with oneness. We are dealing simply with the "inner" nature of that essence.

Christianity and Islam are both monotheistic. They firmly and equally teach that God is one. The conflict is understanding and defining God's divine unity. God's nature surpasses the capacity of our minds to fully grasp or understand. To argue that the Christian belief in God is against reason is simply to make one-self the judge of what God can or cannot be, which is blasphemy.

The non-Christian reader must agree that in using such words as "Father," "Son," and "Holy Spirit," God is using human terms for our benefit. It is God through His grace accommodating Himself to human limitations and ignorance, just as a human father for example must use simple language when trying to explain the computer to a child. There is no human language suitable to express the realities of the Divine Nature. The relationship between the persons of the Godhead so transcends all human thought and language that we can neither comprehend nor express it. Many Muslims state that they cannot believe in the doctrine of the Trinity because they are unable to understand it. In their minds, it has not been proven. However, again, the problem is not in the doctrine itself but in the finiteness of our minds.

Let me pose a question: If an atheist asked for proof for the many beliefs Muslims hold as "truths," would it be possible for you as a Muslim to prove them? For example, consider the Muslim belief in the resurrection of the dead. If an atheist asked you how it would be possible for the dead to be raised back to life, could you satisfactorily explain and prove it? It is not possible to do so through human logic or intellect alone.

My point is that if you allow yourself to reject the tri-unity of God because you cannot understand it or because Christians cannot absolutely prove it with intellectual arguments, then you cannot blame the

atheist for rejecting a belief in God or any other revelation that cannot be absolutely proven. God's essence
is not material but spiritual. God is Spirit and there is
no division in His Spirit. Christians believe that God is
one, who revealed Himself in these three Persons: The
Father, The Son (Jesus, the Word) and the Holy Spirit.

Mankind must accept by faith what God has
revealed about His nature in the Holy Scriptures. For
this reason Christians believe that the persons of the
Trinity are in essence one. Therefore, plurality within
the Trinity does not affect the single essence of God.

According to the Qur'an and the Hadith, Allah has
a face, hands, fingers, feet and eyes (Surah 55:27 and
Surah 38:75). The Muslim scholar AL-Ash'ari wrote:

> "We confess that Allah is firmly seated on His
> Throne...We confess that Allah has two hands,
> without asking how...We confess that Allah
> has two eyes without asking how...We confess
> that Allah has a face...We confirm that Allah
> has knowledge...hearing and sight...and
> power."[109]

And the highly influential Muslim scholar (and
jurist) Imam Abu Hanifah, teaches: "The most high
has a hand and face and soul without asking how."[110]

Human logic and reason alone are insufficient to
lead to the true knowledge of God's nature. "Can you
fathom the mysteries of God? Can you probe the limits
of the Almighty? They are higher than the heavens -
what can you do? They are deeper than the depths of
the grave — what can you know?" (Job 11:7-8). When
we ask why God revealed His Triune nature to us, we

will discover that each Person of the Trinity had an important role to play in our salvation. The Father loves us and gives us many gifts. The most important gift is His Son, Jesus Christ (Isa), who redeemed and saved us. The Holy Spirit regenerates us, empowers us (Acts 1:8), and sanctifies us (Galatians 5:22-23). The Holy Spirit changes us inwardly and enables us to submit to God in obedience because we love Him.

The purpose of God's revelation to us in the Gospel is to guide us to know Him as our Heavenly Father, be forgiven by Him through Jesus Christ, and enjoy His divine presence through the Holy Spirit. God wants us to have the right relationship with Him in order to worship, love and obey Him.

Christian scholar G. Parrinder wrote:

"God as creator and provider is seen in the Father who cares for mankind. The essential nature of God as love manifesting Himself in action is seen in the 'Son,' in the humanity of Christ, his loving actions and words, his suffering and death. The ever-present nature of God is seen in the Spirit. Yet these three are one, the threefold revelation of God to men."[111]

Everyone should believe that God is a loving God. His nature is unchangeable, so the attribute of love must have existed in God from all eternity. Since love must have an object, the question arises: before God created any living being, whom did He love? The answer is clear: In the Divine Unity, there must exist at least a lover and beloved. Only the Christian doctrine of a Triune God explains the existence of the attributes of love in God's divine nature. The God of the Gospel is not singular and totally alone. He is the all sufficient God who is able to exist by Himself in love.

Noted church historian Philip Schaff explains the biblical concept of the Trinity:

> "God is one in three persons [that is, three distinct persons of the same nature], each person expressing the whole fullness of the Godhead with all his attributes...The divine persons are in one another and form a perpetual intercommunication and motion within the divine essence. Each person has all the divine attributes which are inherent in the divine essence but each has also a characteristic individuality or property, which is peculiar to the person,...but the three persons are co-eternal and co-equal."[112]

CHAPTER 26

JESUS IS THE ETERNAL SON OF GOD IN A UNIQUE SPIRITUAL SENSE

THE WAY THE QUR'AN VIEWS JESUS' SONSHIP

Based on many passages in the Qur'an, such as Surah 2:116, Surah 6:101, Surah 9:30, Surah 18:4, and Surah 19:35, many Muslims mistakenly conclude that the Christian belief in the Fatherhood of God and Sonship of Jesus means that God had a consort. They question how, apart from the involvement of a woman, God could beget a son and become a father. Surah 6:101 asks, "...How can He have a son when He hath no consort...?" What Muhammad rejected as untrue was the carnal idea that God had a son through a physical relationship with a partner. Such an idea is blasphemous to Christians, who reject such a notion.

When the Gospel states that Christ is the Son of God, it does not mean that Christ came by procreation. "Son" is not intended to mean a physical relationship or natural birth. It is of another kind: eternal spiritual Sonship (between the Father and the Son) which has no connection with the body or physical propagation. To explain by analogy, it is true that a mind begets thought, but the process of thought conception is not physical.

JESUS' SONSHIP IS NOT BASED ON EARTHLY STANDARDS

When the Gospel reveals Jesus as God the Son, it means God was revealed in His essential nature of love in Christ. As Kenneth Cragg writes: "When we speak of Beethoven the musician, or Leonardo da Vinci the artist, we mean these men and their full personality in a particular capacity. Capacities which do not preclude their having others, but yet involving them wholly."[113]

In physical birth there is a separation (between mother and child), but birth from the Holy Triune God does not involve separation. As Christ said in John 10:30, "I and the Father are One." The Son comes from the Father without leaving Him. Jesus comes out of Him and yet remains in Him. For example, when you think a thought which emerges as sounds, that thought reaches the ears of people yet is still in your mind. It is also possible for the thought to leave your mind and be written on paper and sent to others all over the world. In that sense the thought came out from you and yet it remains in you.

It is revealed through the Word of God that Christ is the Son of God, which means that Christ came from God. We read in the Gospel, "For God so loved the world that He gave his one and only Son, that whoever believes in him shall not perish but have eternal life" (John 3:16). The Gospel clearly teaches that Jesus Christ was the "only begotten Son." The Greek word translated "begotten" in the original text is *monogenae* which means "the one" (mono...) and "coming from" (...genae) or "the one coming from" indicating Jesus came from the Father. Some translators of the Bible translated this word as "only" while others "only begotten." Both are correct because the meaning is the same — the only Son coming from the Father.

Both the Bible and the Qur'an teach as a fact that Jesus was born of a virgin by the will of God, conceived through the power of the Holy Spirit. We know from the Qur'an Jesus is called, "a Spirit from God." According to the Gospel and the Qur'an, Jesus is related to no physical father. He is related to God. If you object to the title "Son of God," can you explain who then is His Father? Note also that we know that God is a Spirit and there is no division in His Spirit.

To reason that God cannot have a son without a wife is the same as reasoning He cannot have life without breath. Although it is true that anything that lives must breathe, God does not breathe and yet He lives.

The word "Son" can be used without indicating sexual union. Allow me to illustrate the principle that we cannot interpret every word in the Bible or the Qur'an in a literal and physical sense.

In the language of Science:

We speak of friction giving birth to heat.

Son in common language:

An Egyptian can be called the "Son of the Nile" because of living near the Nile River in Egypt. An evil person may be called "a Son of Satan."

Son as used in the Qur'an:

The Qur'an, Surah 2:215, calls the person who travels on foot "Ibnu Al Sabil," which means "The Son of the Path." In the Qur'an we read the expression, "Mother of the Book" (Surah 13:39). Does that mean that there are children of the Book?

Muhammad makes an amazing statement about worship if Allah had a son in Surah 43:81, "Say: 'If (Allah) Most gracious had a son, I would be the first to worship.'" "The prophet of Allah does not object to true worship in any form. But it must be true:...."[114] Note that the Qur'an, in this verse, does not teach the absolute impossibility for God to have a Son.

Surah 19:35 states "It is not befitting to (the majesty of) Allah that He should beget a Son." The meaning of this verse is that having a Son does not glorify God.

JESUS CLEARLY TEACHES THAT HE IS THE "SON OF GOD"

It is very clear from Scripture that Jesus is the absolute, eternal, unique, divine Son of God. The very title, "Son of God" immediately suggests Jesus' specific function. An earthly father and his son are fully human and have the same sinful human nature, yet the son is always subject to his father. Likewise, the expression "the Son of God" indicates the relationship between the first two Persons of the Triune God. Jesus and the Father share the same divine nature, yet Jesus subjected *Himself* to the authority of the Father. When Jesus came to earth, He came to do His Father's will and to glorify His Heavenly Father. The expression "Son of God" indicates likeness or sameness of nature.

The title "Son of God" expresses the close relationship of Christ to God in the divine self-revelation. "In him [Jesus] dwelt all the fullness (pleroma) of the godhead bodily" (Colossians 2:9). Jesus is the visible expression of the invisible God.

Let's examine Jesus' claims to be the Son of God, who submits to the will of His Father, as illustrated in the Gospel in "The Parable of the Tenants and the Vineyard." In Luke 20:9-16, Jesus speaks of Himself in the Parable of the Tenants of the Vineyard:

> "He (Jesus) went on to tell the people this parable: A man planted a vineyard, rented it to some farmers and went away for a long time. At harvest time he sent a servant to the tenants so they would give him some of the fruit of the vineyard. But the tenants beat him and sent him away empty-handed. He sent another servant, but that one also they beat and treated shamefully and sent away empty-handed. He sent still a third, and they wounded him and threw him out. Then the owner of the vineyard said, 'What shall I do? I will send my son, whom I love; perhaps they will respect him.' But when the tenants saw him, they talked the matter over. 'This is the heir,' they said. 'Let's kill him, and the inheritance will be ours.' So they threw him out of the vineyard and killed him. What then will the owner of the vineyard do to them? He will come and kill those tenants and give the vineyard to others. When the people (the religious leaders at the time) heard this, they said, 'May this never be!' "

The main elements in this parable are the following:

- The owner of the vineyard is God, the one who planted the vineyard.

- The vineyard is the nation of Israel.

- The tenants are the Jewish religious leaders.

- The landowner's servants are the prophets who were sent to the nation of Israel.

- The landowner's son is Jesus Christ, the Messiah.

In the parable, Jesus claims to be sent from the owner of the vineyard as his son, and those in charge of tending the vineyards killed the owner's son. The Jewish leaders clearly understood what He was saying, for in the next few verses it is reported that: "The teachers of the law and the chief priests looked for a way to arrest him immediately, because they knew he had spoken this parable against them. But they were afraid of the people" (Luke 20:19). They wanted to kill Jesus because He claimed to be the Son of God.

The clear interpretation of this parable is that God sent many prophets to the people of Israel to ask them to produce the "good fruits" of righteousness. The Jewish leadership rejected the prophets and treated them badly. After God the Father sent the prophets, He sent His Only Beloved Son—and the Jewish people rejected and then killed Him. Jesus was sent by the Father to the vineyard, and He went in submission to His Father's will. Although it led to His death, Jesus' life and work was entirely to the Glory of God.

JESUS CONFRONTS THE JEWISH RELIGIOUS LEADERS:

In John 10:36-39, Jesus referred to Himself as the Son of God: "What about the one whom the Father set apart as his very own and sent into the world? Why then do you accuse me of blasphemy because I said, 'I am God's Son?' Do not believe me unless I do what my Father does. But if I do it, even though you do not believe me, believe the miracles, that you may know and understand that the Father is in me, and I in the Father. Again they [the religious leaders at the time] tried to seize him..."

This is just one example of Jesus' claims to be the divine Son of God. For further references, see Matthew 17:5, and John 5:16-18. Ultimately, it was His claim to be the Son of God that caused the Jews to have Him crucified (Matthew 26:63-65; Mark 14:61-63; Luke 22:70 and John 19:7).

SECTION TEN

WHAT KIND OF GOD RULES THE UNIVERSE?

CHAPTER 27

MUHAMMAD'S OWN TESTIMONY

Ibn Ishaq* quoted a letter sent by Muhammad to the Negus of Abyssinia. In it, Muhammad wrote, "I bear witness that Jesus, son of Mary, is the Spirit of God and His Word, which he cast to Mary the virgin."[115] The title "Word of God" here is a title describing Jesus and His mission.

According to the teaching of the Muslim scholars, Jesus is the only prophet who was believed upon while still in his mother's womb. The Muslim commentators agree that the prophet Yahya (John the Baptist) was the first to believe that Jesus is the Word of God. The famous Muslim scholar Al Razi commented on Surah 3:39, which states "...Yahya witnessing the truth of a Word from Allah..." Razi explained: "What is meant by 'Word of God' is Isa, peace be upon him. This is the choice of the majority of the commentators."[116]

The following story is reported by a well-known early Muslim historian, Ibn Kathir: "...the mother of Jesus met the mother of Yahya, peace be upon them. Both were pregnant, one with Jesus, the other with Yahya. Yahya's mother said to Mary, "Do you feel I am pregnant?" Mary said, "I am also pregnant." The wife of Zekaraiah said, "I found that he who is inside me bows down to the one inside of you." Ibn Kathir wrote:

---

*Ibn Ishaq was an early Islamic Scholar. He left behind two comprehensive works on the life of Muhamad. His work is still considered today an essential source for everyone who wants to learn about Muhamad's life and his companions.

"This is what is meant by John's confirming (or believing in) the Word of God which is Jesus, found in the Qur'an, Surah 3:39. 'John who shall confirm a Word from God.' "[117]

According to the most reliable Islamic records, Ibn Abbas was the most informed person among the Muslim people as to what God revealed to Muhammad. It is well known among learned Muslim scholars that Muhammad prompted his adherents to learn the Qur'an from Ibn Abbas. Ibn Abbas was the official interpreter of the Islamic Law during the era of the two Caliphs, Umar Ibn Al-Khattab and Uthman Ibn Affan. Umar Ibn AL-Khattab used to say that the interpreter of the Qur'an is Ibn Abbas.[118] Ibn Abbas made known the early belief that the appropriate response to Jesus being the Word of God is to bow down to him and that the prophet Yahya was the first to acknowledge that Jesus is the Word of God. Ibn Abbas said, "His bowing down to Jesus in His mother's womb was his expression of faith in Jesus."[119]

Ibn Abbas further said, "Yahya's bowing down in his mother's womb is his believing that Jesus is the Word of God."[120] Ibn Abbas said that Yahya was the first to believe and confirm that Jesus is "the Word of God" and "His Spirit."[121] Yahya bowed down to Jesus even though he was an eminent and prominent prophet according to the Qur'an and the Bible.

My dear Muslim friend, bowing down is a clear and strong form of worship. Worship is due only to God, who has no partner. The prophet Yahya's bowing down to Jesus as the Word of God means that Jesus is the Eternal, uncreated, Divine Word of God because the prophet Yahya would not have bowed down to Jesus if Jesus was created. Otherwise, the prophet would be committing "shirk," the sin of associating another with God. Yahya was six months in the womb when he bowed down to Jesus. Actually, it was God who inspired and moved Yahya to bow down to Jesus. This, my Muslim friend, is a clear confirmation from God Himself that Jesus is indeed His eternal Word. The Gospel agrees with this original Islamic belief that Jesus is worthy to receive worship. Some examples are illustrated in the following scriptures: Matthew 9:18, Matthew 14:33, Matthew 28:9, Matthew 28:17 and John 9:35-38 .

In addition, the great Muslim scholar Al Razi explains why the prophet Yahya was given his name. The name "Yahya" is taken from the verb "alive." Al Razi said, "Yahya was the first to believe in Jesus, so his heart became alive by that faith."[122] Isn't that wonderful! The great prophet Yahya's heart was made alive by his faith in Jesus.

True followers of Jesus know that only God and His Word are able to give life to a dead spirit. Only God and His Word can cause a person to be born again and thus be spiritually alive. My dear Muslim reader, if you believe and worship Jesus as the Divine Word of God, you will be following the example of the prominent prophet Yahya. You will be in harmony with the testimony and work of God who inspired and moved the prophet Yahya in his mother's womb to bow down to Jesus. Philippians 2:9-11 informs us, "Therefore God exalted him to the highest place and gave him the name that is above every name, that at the name of

Jesus every knee should bow, in heaven and on earth and under the earth, and every tongue confess that Jesus Christ is Lord, to the glory of God the Father."

My dear friend, all the facts that I shared with you in this book were never intended by God to be only for one special group of people. Understanding and personally applying this truth is a common right for all humanity to become spiritually enlightened and alive!

CHAPTER 28
GOD IS LOVE

WHAT IS THE PERFECT FORM OF WORSHIP?

A Jewish teacher asked Jesus, "...'Teacher, which is the greatest commandment in the Law?' Jesus replied: 'Love the Lord your God with all your heart and with all your soul and with all your mind.' This is the first and greatest commandment" (Matthew 22:35-38). Jesus taught us that loving God with all our heart, soul and mind is what God requires of us in worshipping Him. Jesus also taught us that if we truly love God, we will express our love through obedience to Him. "Whoever has my commands and obeys them, he is the one who loves me" (John 14:21). God in the Gospel is not just asking us to obey His commandments, but He is asking us first to love Him with all our heart, soul, and mind. And as a natural result we will want to obey Him. Loving God the way Jesus taught us means practically surrendering, giving ourselves totally to Him, and living everyday of our lives for Him, to please Him.

God knows that the mere performance of religious duties does not automatically show that we love Him. Nor does it necessarily mean that we are totally submissive to Him. For it is possible for someone to perform all the religious duties while his heart and mind is not dedicated completely in submission to God. Our bodies can bow to God while our hearts can at the same time rebel against God. People may try to obey and serve God out of fear, habit, pride, or prospect of reward. Therefore, my dear friend, Jesus' words recorded in the Gospel of Matthew reveal the mind and will of God. There is no higher or better form of worship that we could offer to God than to love Him with all our heart, soul, and mind, as Jesus taught. This is the perfect form of worship which pleases our Creator.

Let us consider two important questions every reasonable person has the right to ask about God. First, is it possible for me to love God with all my heart, soul and mind? Second, is the God who asks for such love, worthy of such love? The answer to these questions involves three important issues:

- What is my relationship to God?

- Did God express His love for me in a strong way?

- Can I experience God's love for me in my own heart?

My dear friend, certain essential conditions must be present before you can truly be able to *love* God:

Love must be genuine:

For your love to be genuine toward God, you must first experience in your heart His perfect and eternal forgiveness. Then your heart will be free from fear and you will be able to love Him. The man who has no assurance of forgiveness from God could not possibly serve God and keep His commandments out of genuine love. Rather, he would obey Him with the primary objective of trying to obtain His forgiveness and trying to reduce His wrath.

Love must be full of expression:

For your love to be expressive toward God, you need to see the very best of God's love. Your expression of love toward God can only be in response to and in gratitude for the manifestation of God's love toward you. Those who see and understand more of God's prefect love toward them will respond in a more fervent way in love toward God.

Love must be mutual:

For your love toward God to be mutual, God must enable you to have the fullest possible experience of His love in your own heart. This way you can have the natural inclination from within your soul to love Him.

THE LOVE OF GOD IN THE QUR'AN

What does the Qur'an say about the Love of God? The answer to this question involves the same three important issues: What is the believer's relationship to Allah? Did Allah express His love for the believer in a personal way? Can I experience Allah's love for me in my own heart? Let us examine each of these points.

Love must be genuine:

In Surah 23:60, we read the following, "And those who dispense their charity with their hearts full of fear, because they will return to their Lord." Muhammad himself explained what is meant by that verse. "A'isha said, 'O, apostle of God, is the one who is afraid of God the one who commits adultery, steals, drinks wine, thus he is afraid of punishment?' Muhammad told her, 'No, O daughter of Sedik, he is the one who prays, fasts and gives alms, thus he is afraid that God may not accept these things from him.' "[123]

The Qur'an states: "Not one of the beings in the heavens and the earth but must come to (Allah) Most Gracious as a servant" (Surah 19:93). The word servant in this verse is an incorrect translation to the Arabic word "Abd," which only can mean slave. God (Allah) in the Qur'an is the Master, and the "believer" is only a slave (Abd) or at best a servant. Genuine love cannot come from the attitude of a slave. The slave does not work for the master's sake but primarily works for his own benefits and rewards. The Muslim believer's acceptance by Allah depends entirely on the believer's performance; nevertheless, God has the right to dismiss him because he is the Master. This relationship is not conducive to love. Genuine love cannot come from a servant/slave mentality.

God in the Qur'an is most commonly known as a judge who never promises complete forgiveness to the believers nor does he guarantee them eternal life in Paradise. For this reason, it is impossible for the Muslim believer to enjoy real peace in his heart. He cannot be free from fear when he knows that God's judgement could be against him. Surah 5:18 states about God, "...He forgiveth whom He pleaseth and He punisheth whom He pleaseth..." Note: The English word punisheth in this verse is the incorrect translation of the original Arabic word "uazebo." The word "uazebo" can only mean "torture."

The Muslim believer cannot love God for God's sake but for his own sake, to alleviate God's wrath and try to gain His forgiveness and acceptance. However, genuine love must be the exercise of the purest affections of the heart toward God. Naturally, God desires a free response of love from those who worship Him.

Love must be full of expression:

My dear friend, the Qur'an has very little to say about God's expression of love to you and me. The Qur'an does not tell us of any great act of love in the history of God's dealings with mankind. The Qur'an is silent about any deep and strong feelings of love God may have toward us. Throughout the pages of the Qur'an, we do not see any mention or demonstration of God's full measure of love toward us.

Love must be mutual:

It is not possible, according to the Qur'an, for you or me to actually experience God's love in our very own hearts. We read in the Qur'an numerous names given to God: "He is Allah...to Him belong the Most beautiful names..." (Surah 59:24). According to Muslim scholars, there are ninety-nine beautiful names of God in the Qur'an. Note that not one of these beautiful names is "the Father" or "God is Love." The closest name to indicate kindness in the Qur'an is "AL-Wadud" (Surah 85:14), which means "The Kind or Amicable One." It is well-known that this name, "AL-Wadud," does not reveal the essential quality of love which is self-sacrifice.

One of the most famous and greatest Muslim theologians in Islamic history, AL-Ghazzali, explains that the expression "AL-Wadud" means far less than the title would seem to indicate. He wrote a book about the ninety-nine names of Allah, *AL-Maqsad al-Asna*, in which he states that this title "AL-Wadud" in the Qur'an is a lesser one for example than the title "The Merciful" ("AL-Rahim"). All Muslim scholars agree with his opinion. For God is called "the Merciful" over a hundred times in the Qur'an, but is called "AL-Wadud" only twice (Surah 11:90 and Surah 85:14).

It is indisputable that love is much stronger, richer, and deeper than mercy. Love is the best virtue and characteristic that anyone could have. You can show mercy to a poor man by giving him a few dollars or something to eat, but you love your children and sacrifice for them.

AL-Ghazzali explains God's (Allah's) love as consisting solely of objective acts of kindness and expressions of approval. He denies that there is any subjectivity in the love of God. He denies that God feels any love in His own heart toward mankind. AL-Ghazzali states, "God remains above the feeling of love."[124] He confirms this unfortunate fact in the Qur'an by saying of God's love, "Love and Mercy are desired in respect of their objects only for the sake of their fruit and benefit and not because of empathy or feeling."[125] In other words, when Allah says he loves you, what He means is He will show mercy to you by giving you good things, but you must not interpret that to mean that He feels anything in His heart for you.

My Muslim friend, the God whom the Qur'an depicts and introduces to us does not satisfy the thirst and longing of our souls. He cannot give rest or joy to our wandering hearts. For instance, a woman knew a man and wanted to spend the rest of her life with him. Unfortunately, this man only bestowed gifts on her if and when she pleased him. He absolutely refused to let her know whether or not he loved her. He refused to marry her. He wouldn't even guarantee that he would always be with her. This man wanted her only to be his servant. I ask you, if you were that woman, how would you feel? Would you feel loved?

Therefore, it is impossible for the Muslim to give God the most perfect form of worship, which is loving Him with all his heart, soul, and mind. He is unable to express such love to God through his joyful and willing submission (obedience) to His commandments.

THE LOVE OF GOD IN THE GOSPEL

In comparison, the God of the Gospel makes it possible for us to give Him the most perfect form of worship because:

• God allows us to enter into a wonderful relationship with Him. This relationship entitles us to become His children. "Yet to all who received Him (Jesus), to those who believed in his name, He gave the right to become children of God. Children born not of natural descent, nor of human decision or a husband's will, but born of God" (John 1:12-13). In the Bible, God is most commonly called "The Father."

"How great is the love the Father has lavished on us, that we should be called children of God..." 1 John 3:1.

God draws near to us as a loving father draws near to his children.

As a concerned father He disciplines us in love with the purpose of correcting us.

Love and forgiveness always characterizes His relationship with us.

Heaven is our home because He made us His children. "Do not be afraid, little flock, for your Father has been pleased to give you the kingdom" (Luke 12:32). We as true followers of Christ are certain of God's good will towards us.

• God gave us His Son. "But God demonstrates his own love for us in this: While we were still sinners, Christ died for us" (Romans 5:8). God has done the greatest thing he could possibly do to reveal His deep, strong, and perfect love for you and me (John 15:13).

• God gives us the Holy Spirit who indwells us and makes us conscious of God's love toward us.

Through the Holy Spirit, who takes residence in our hearts the moment we put our faith in Christ as our Savior, we are able to actually experience God's Fatherly love for us within our hearts and souls. Romans 5:5 promises, "And hope does not disappoint us, because God has poured out his love into our hearts by the Holy Spirit, whom he has given us."

This is one of the most glorious truths in the Gospel. We are adopted children of God through Jesus Christ. We experience this relationship through the Holy Spirit as explained in the Gospel. "But when the time had fully come, God sent his Son, born of a woman, born under law, to redeem those under law, that we might receive the full right of sonship. Because you are sons, God sent the Spirit of his Son into our hearts, the Spirit who calls out, 'Abba, Father' " (Galatians 4:4-6). God sent the Spirit of His Son into our hearts to make us aware within our hearts that God is our heavenly Father and we are His children. We read in the Bible, in Romans 8:15-16: "For you did not receive a spirit that makes you a slave again to fear, but you received the Spirit of sonship. And by him we cry, 'Abba, Father.' The Spirit himself testifies with our spirit that we are God's children."

I remember clearly the time I put my faith in Jesus. I felt that God was embracing me and giving me a big hug. Because of what Jesus has done for us, we can be pardoned from our condemned criminal status and can enter the family of God as beloved children. This change occurs the very moment that we accept Him and decide to follow Him. This is the way that God made it possible for us to be elevated to the highest level as His beloved children!

The love of the Father for you, my dear Muslim friend, made manifest in Jesus Christ, becomes your own personal possession through the Holy Spirit at the moment you believe in Jesus as your personal Savior. My sole purpose for writing this book is to help you experience in your own heart God's deep love for you. You can know God as your heavenly Father by being born again of His Divine Spirit. The moment you accept the Messiah, Jesus, as your Savior and Lord, you are born again spiritually and you will experience the heavenly Father's loving arms drawing you to His bosom.

The true followers of Jesus can look up toward God and say from all their grateful hearts, "There is no limit to the potential of my love for You."

CONCLUSION IN COMPARING THE LOVE OF GOD IN CHRISTIANITY AND ISLAM.

Typically a servant must work to earn his place in a home, and even then stays outside in the servant's assigned place. The servant always strives to obtain his master's approval and is afraid to be dismissed. The master has the freedom to dismiss his servant at any time. Unlike servants, true Christians are God's children. As Christians, we look to a Father whose kingdom is our home, and we rejoice in our hope of inheriting and sharing His glory.

When the true Christian believer thinks about God, he finds himself drawn with the most awesome attraction. God's love for us is irresistible. His love captures our hearts.

We can clearly see in this chapter the superiority of the Christian faith:

• God in the Gospel has the most wonderful and perfect character. We Christians stand in awe when we see the magnitude of God's marvelous love toward us.

• Jesus in the Bible commanded the believers to give God the most perfect form of worship. It makes sense that the Creator requires His creatures to give Him their best, that is themselves.

• God made it possible for believers to give Him perfect worship, as expressed in this chapter.

As author of this book, I can easily say I am in love with Him after all that God has done for me and in me. He is worthy of my life and my affection. I love Him with all my heart. I want to seek Him, to know Him more closely, to serve Him more, and to praise Him. My pleasure and satisfaction is found in giving Him every day of my life.

These are not empty words or theories. They are God's truth. To prove to you that God means what He says in the Gospel, you can experience Him in your life as your loving heavenly Father. You can feel in your heart His embrace and enjoy His very presence within you if you go to Him through Jesus Christ. If you step out by faith and believe that Jesus Christ died for your sins and go to God to ask His forgiveness, He will forgive all your sins, enter your life, and you will experience His wonderful peace and love immediately right where you are.

Understanding and personally acting upon all of the facts from the Qur'an and the Bible which I have presented in this book is a God-given opportunity for anyone and everyone to know Him and experience His love and salvation!

CHAPTER 29

JESUS IS UNIQUE BECAUSE HE IS OUR SAVIOR

Again the problem is that sin is an integral part of the human nature. All kinds of iniquity dwells in the human heart: lust, envy, greed, pride, hatred, selfishness, and other traits associated with a fallen creature. The human body is the breeding ground and playground of sin. Sin has a vicious control within. All human bodies have been captive to the power of sin.

The Gospel tells us that the only one who is pure from sin is Jesus. He came, "...in the likeness of sinful flesh...He condemned sin in the flesh..." (Romans 8:3, NKJ).

The Good News of the Gospel is that Jesus came and defeated the power of sin in its own dwelling place, the human body. He had complete victory over all of Satan's temptations and He lived without committing one single sin. Jesus' divine nature guaranteed His victory in the battle against Satan and sin. Jesus won the battle on our behalf.

The Good News of the Gospel is that God made it possible for you to be united with Jesus through the Holy Spirit, who will reside within you at the very moment you place your faith in Jesus as your Savior. As a natural consequence of being united with Him, you will enjoy the fruits of His victory. You will experience for the first time in your life victory over Satan and over sin. Jesus said: "...everyone who sins is a slave to sin" (John 8:34). He further said: "So if the Son sets you free, you will be free indeed" (John 8:36). The Good News of the Gospel is that the Son of God came as the unique man, Jesus, to save you and set you free from the love and captivity of sin. You see now my friend, Jesus Christ came to do what the law and prophets could not do. "The reason the Son of God appeared was to destroy the devil's work" (1 John 3:8). Jesus declared, "If you do not believe that I am the one I claim to be, you will indeed die in your sins" (John 8:24).

Jesus also came and suffered the most horrible consequence for our sin - death. Jesus endured the cross on our behalf. Jesus suffered the wrath of God toward sin. Jesus identified with the sin and death of every person when he died on the cross. Legally, God looks at us (true believers) as if we had died with Christ. The Good News of the Bible is that Jesus came to save us and set us free from paying the penalty for our sins. The penalty has been paid. According to the principle of double jeopardy, the person cannot be tried twice for the same crime.

The Wonderful News of the Gospel is that the moment you believe in Jesus as your Savior, you will be united with Him and also will experience for the first time in your life, right within your heart, the forgiveness of God for all your sins. You will enjoy the wonderful peace with God. The Good News of the Gospel is Jesus came and bridged the gap between heaven and earth. Jesus came to reconcile sinful man with the Holy God.

The Wonderful News of the Gospel is Jesus came and conquered death itself. When Jesus rose from the dead to be with God, He declared victory over death. Jesus reversed the worst consequence of sin, which is eternal separation from God's presence. Christ's resurrection is the first in a long line of resurrections to come of those who believe in Him. We read, "But Christ has indeed been raised from the dead, the first fruits of those who have fallen asleep" (1 Corinthians 15:20).

The Wonderful News of the Gospel is that the moment you believe that Jesus died for your sins and turn to God in repentance, God's Holy Spirit will come to dwell within you and will assure you that you are now going to heaven. Paradise will become your home and your destiny. "If we have been united with Him like this in His death, we will certainly also be united with Him in his resurrection" (Romans 6:5). (See also 1 Peter 1:3,4).

The reason that you will know for sure that you are going to heaven is that the same Jesus who lives in heaven will come to live in you through the Holy Spirit. God's Word declares, "And if the Spirit of him who raised Jesus from the dead is living in you, he who raised Christ from the dead will also give life to your mortal bodies through his Spirit, who lives in you" (Romans 8:11). We read in the Bible, Galatians 4:6-7: "Because you are sons, God sent the Spirit of His Son into our hearts, the Spirit who calls out, 'Abba, Father.' So you are no longer a slave, but a son; and since you are a son, God has made you also an heir." The living and life-giving Spirit of Christ imparts to you eternal life. Jesus told us in the Gospel, "…Because I live, you also will live" (John 14:19).

When Jesus ascended to heaven, he returned to heaven as a human being and as a Divine eternal spirit. His presence in heaven as a human being is our assurance that we too one day will go there. You see now my Muslim friend why the Son of God came as the unique man Jesus. He is our Savior because He fully bridged the gap between heaven (God) and earth (man). For this reason, the Gospel declares, "Salvation is found in no one else, for there is no other name under heaven given to men by which we must be saved" (Acts 4:12). Jesus states clearly, "I am the gate; whoever enters through me will be saved" (John 10:9). Jesus further declares, "I am the way and the truth and the life. No one comes to the Father except through me" (John 14:6).

Jesus said, "I have come that they may have life, and have it to the full" (John 10:10). God has created us in such a way that we will never be satisfied, have a sense of completeness, or enjoy our life fully until we have the right relationship with Him. Then we will experience His presence and Salvation in our lives in a very real and personal way. "But because Jesus lives forever...He is able to save completely those who come to God through Him, because He always lives to intercede for them" (Hebrews 7:24-25).

WHAT IS YOUR DECISION?

Jesus spoke to all people through the Gospel. He spoke to you, my Muslim friend, because He loves you. Jesus promised, "Come to me, all you who are weary and burdened, and I will give you rest" (Matthew 11:28).

Jesus also declared that He can satisfy your deepest spiritual longing. "He said, 'I am the bread of life. He who comes to me will never go hungry, and he who believes in me will never be thirsty' " (John 6:35). "Jesus stood and said in a loud voice, 'If anyone is thirsty, let him come to me and drink' " (John 7:37).

Jesus *Himself*, is the "light" for those who seek Him. Jesus wants to guide you, and help you discover the purpose of your life. "When Jesus spoke again to the people, he said, 'I am the light of the world. Whoever follows me will never walk in darkness, but will have the light of life' " (John 8:12).

Jesus said, "Most assuredly, I say to you, he who believes in Me has everlasting life" (John 6:47, NKJ). My dear friend, my purpose for writing this book is to help you discover that *love is the supreme attribute of God*. I urge you to believe God's Word and take a step by faith. I can't adequately describe or define God's deep and everlasting love for you. I know from personal experience that the moment you believe in Jesus, you too will actually experience and taste within your heart and soul His great and wonderful love for you. God wants to make you joyful and satisfied. He desires to fill your life with joy, love, hope, and peace. God desires to have fellowship with you. Through this fellowship, God accomplishes His perfect will. God said: "...I have loved you with an everlasting love; I have drawn you with loving-kindness " (Jeremiah 31:3).

My friend, God yearns for your companionship. He chose *you* — now the choice is *yours*. Romans 10:8-9 tells us clearly: "The word is near you; it is in your mouth and in your heart, that is, the word of faith we are proclaiming: That if you confess with your mouth, 'Jesus is Lord,' and believe in your heart that God raised him from the dead, you will be saved." Your salvation depends on your decision. If you choose to put your faith in Jesus as your Lord and Savior, here is a suggested personal and specific prayer. Pray it if you mean it with all your heart:

> *"God, I know that I am a sinner. Thank you Jesus for taking my place and dying on the cross for my sins. Jesus, I ask you to come into my life, cleanse me of my sin, be my Savior, be my Lord, and help me to walk with God, and submit to His will."*

If you prayed this prayer, let me be the first one to welcome you into God's eternal family. I would like to congratulate you on having made the best and most important decision of your life and receiving the miracle of eternal life with God.

BIBLIOGRAPHY

No author. *Behind the Veil,* Unmasking Islam, American C.F. Association, Burke, Virginia USA (no date)

Abdul-Haqq. Abdiyah Akbar. *Christ in the New Testament and the Qur'an*, Abdul-Haqq, Evanston, USA (1975)

Abdul-Haqq. Abdiyah Akbar. *Sharing Your Faith With a Muslim*, Bethany Fellowship, Minneapolis, USA (1980)

Abi Hanifah. Imam, *Al-Fiqh al-Akbar*, Dar al-Kutub al-Elmeyah, Beirut (1979)

Al-Ahadith Al-Qudsiyyah. Divine Narratives, Translated by Dr. Abdul Khaliqkazi and Dr. Alan B. Day, Dar Al-Iman Publishing House, Tripoli-Lebanon (no date)

Alam, Maulana Syed Mohammad Badre. *Descension of Jesus Christ*, Dini Book, Urdu Bazaar, Dehli, India (1974)

ALIM. Release 4.5, ISL Software Corporation (1996) — *The Hadith*

Ali, Abdullah Yusuf. *The Meaning of the Holy Qur'an*, Eighth Edition, amana publications, Beltsville, Maryland, USA (1996)

Kramers, J.H. *Shorter Encyclopedia of Islam*, (publishing house not noted), New York, New York, USA (1961)

Anderson, M. *Jesus, the Light and Fragrance of God*; Three Volumes, Pioneer Book Company, Caney, Kansas, USA (1994)

Anderson, M. *The Trinity*; Pioneer Book Company, Caney, Kansas, USA (1994)

Arberry, A.J. *Revelation and Reason in Islam*, George Allen & Unwin Ltd., London, United Kingdom (no date)

Assfy, Z. *Islam and Christianity*, William Sessions Ltd., York, United Kingdom (1977)

Bevan, J. *Christianity Explained to Muslims*, YMCA Publishing House, Calcutta, India (1952)

Boice, James Montgomery. *Foundations of the Christian Faith*; Intervarsity Press, Oowners Grove, Illinois, USA (1981)

Brown, D. *The Divine Trinity, Christianity and Islam*, Sheldon Press, London, United Kingdom (1967)

Broyles, C.C. "The Redeeming King: Psalm 72's Contribution to the Messianic Ideal," in Evans, C.A. and Flint, P.W., *Eschatology, Messianism and the Dead Sea Scrolls*, ed., Williams B. Eerdmans Publishing Company, Grand Rapids, Michigan USA (1997)

Bhai, Abdullah. *AL-Masih - the Anointed One*; CMM, Springfield, Missouri, USA (no date)

Burrows, Millar. *The Dead Sea Scrolls*, The Viking Press, New York, New York, USA (1955)

Chapman, Colin. *You Go and Do the Same: Studies in Relating to Muslims*, CMS, London, United Kingdom, 1983.

Cragg, K. *Jesus and the Muslim*, George, Allen and Unwin, London, United Kingdom (1985)

Crawford, Craig. *The Prophecies: A Journey to the End of Time*, Prophecy Press (1999)

Durrani, M.H. Dr. *The Qur'anic Facts About Jesus*, International Islamic Publishers, Karachi, Pakistan (1983)

Enns, Paul P. *The Moody Handbook of Theology*; Moody Press, Chicago, USA (1989)

Ersen, Ishak. *Jesus Christ in the Traditions of Islam*; Light of Life, Villach, Austria (1992)

Fadi, Abd al. *Sin and Atonement in Islam and Christianity*, Markaz-ash-Shabiba, Beirut, Lebanon (no date)

Ghabril, Nicola Yacob. *Themes for the Diligent; The Good Way*, Rikon, Switzerland (no date)

Gilchrist, John. *The Christian Witness to Muslims*; Roodepoort Mission Press, Roodepoort, Republic ofSouth Africa (1988)

Goldsack, W. *Christ in Islam*, The Christian Literature Society, Madras, India (1905)

Guillaume, A. *Life of Muhammad*, A Translation of Ibn Ishaq's SIRAT ARASUL, London, United Kingdom (1955)

Hahn, E. *Jesus in Islam*, (publishing house not available), Vaniyamki, India (1975)

Hanifah, Imam Abi. *Al-Fiqh al-Akbar*, Dar AL-Kutub al-elmeyah, Beirut, Lebanon (1997)

Harman, Henry, M. *Introduction to the Study of the Holy Scriptures*; Volume I, Hunt and Eaton, New York, New York, USA (1878)

Halverson, Dean C. (general editor), *The Compact Guide to World Religions*, International Students, Inc., Bethany House Publishers, Minneapolis, Minnesota, USA (1996)

Imran, Maulana Muhammad. *The Teachings of Jesus in the Light of A-Qur'an*, Malik Sirajudden and Sons, Kashmiri Bazar, Lahore, Pakistan (1980)

Jadeed, Iskander. *The Cross in the Gospel and Qur'an*, Markaz-ash-Shabiba, Beirut, Lebanon (no date)

Jadeed, Iskander. *Did God Appear in the Flesh?*, The Good Way, Rikon, Switzerland (no date)

Jadeed, Iskander. *How to Share the Gospel with Our Muslim Brothers.* Light of Life, Villach, Austria (no date)

Jalalan, AL. Commentary of AL Jalalan, Al Azhar - supervision (1983)

Josephus, Flavius. *The Complete Works of Josephus*, translated by Whitson, W., edition 1981 (original translation dated 1960), Kregel Publications, Grand Rapids, Michigan, USA (1981)

Kateregga, Badru D. and Shenk, David W., *Islam and Christianity*; Uzima Press Ltd., Kenya (1980)

Khalid Muhammad Khalid. *The Successor of the Prophet*, Dar Thabet (1986)

Khaliqkazi, Abdul, Dr. and Day, A.B., Dr. *Al-Ahadith AL-Qudsiyyah*, Dar Al-Iman Publishing House, Tripoli-Lebanon (no date)

Larson, Gary N. *The New Unger's Bible Handbook*, revised, Moody Press, London, United Kingdom (1984)

Maurer, Andreas. *Illustrations, Parables and Stories*; MERCSA, Mondeor, Republic of South Africa (1994)

Morin, Harry. *Responding to Muslims*; CMM, Springfield, Missouri, USA (1994)

Nurbakhash, Javad. *Jesus in the Eyes of the Sufis*, Khaniqahi-Nimatullahi Publications, London, United Kingdom (1983)

Obaray, A.H. *Miraculous Conception, Death, Resurrection and Ascension of Jesus as Taught in the Kuran*, Kimberley, Republic of South Africa (1962)

Orethke, J.P. *A Christian Approach to Muslims*, William Carey Library, Pasadena, USA (1979)

Parrinder, G. *Jesus in the Qur'an*, Oxford University Press, New York, New York, USA (1977)

Payne, J. Barton, *Encyclopedia of Biblical Prophecy*, Fifth Edition, Baker Book House, Grand Rapids, Michigan, USA (1987)

Pfander, C.G. *Balance of Truth*; Light of Life, Villach, Austria (1986)

Qaradawi, al-. Yousef, Elewah Mostafa and Ali Gammar, *t-Twahid*, Qatar, (1968)

Register, R.G. *Dialogue and Interfaith Witness with Muslims*, Moody Books, Inc., Chicago, Illinois, USA (1979)

Robertson, K.G. *Jesus or Isa*, Vantage Press, New York, New York, USA (1983)

Robson, J. *Christ in Islam*, John Murray, London, United Kingdom (1929)

Ryrie, Charles C. *Basic Theology*; Moody Press, Wheaton Illinois, USA (1981)

Schaff, Philip. *The Creeds of Christendom: with a History and Critical Notes*, in, Schaff, David, S., ed., *The History of the Creeds*, Volume 1, Baker Book House, Grand Rapids, Michigan, USA (1983)

Shahid, Dr. Samuel. *The Fallen Nature of Man in Islam and Christianity*; AL-Nour, Colorado Springs, Colorado, USA (1989)

Smith, Chuck. *Answers for Today*, Word for Today, The Word for Today, Costa Mesa, California, USA (1993)

Smith, John Pye. *The Scripture Testimony to the Messiah*, William Oliphant and Company, Edinburgh, Scotland (1859)

Stade, R. *Ninety-Nine Names of God in Islam*, Daystar Press, Ibadan, Nigeria (1970)

Suyuti, AL-. *The Right in Qur'an's Science (AL-Itqan)*, Dar Al Torth (the Traditions) Abo-Al-Fadi (no date)

Tabari, AL-. *Ta'rikh ar-rusul wa'l - mu luk*, Leyde, Volume 1 (1879 revised 1901)

Tabari, Ali. *The Book of Religion and Empire*. Law Publishing Company, Lahore, Pakistan.

Tisdail, William St. Clair. *Christian Reply to Muslim Objections*; Light of Life, Villach, Austria (1904)

Walfson, Harry Austryn. *The Philosophy of the Kalam*, Harvard University Press (1976)

Wismer, D. *The Islamic Jesus*, Gerland Publishing, Inc., New York, New York, USA (1977)

Zwemer, S. *The Moslem Doctrine of God*, Oliphant,Anderson and Ferrier, London, United Kingdom (1905)

Zwemer, S. *The Moslem Christ*, Oliphant, Anderson and Ferrier, London, United Kingdom (1912)

NOTES

1. Chapman, Colin. *You Go and Do the Same: Studies in Relating to Muslims*. CMS, London, United Kingdom, 1983.
2. *Islam and Chrisitanity*, Shenk and Kateregga, pp. 109+
3. *Sahih AL-Bukhari*, 6:477 (see also 6:77)
4. Ibn Abi Dawud, *Kitab al-Masahif*, pp. 23 &83.
5. *Sahih AL-Bukhari*, 6:478
6. *Sahih AL-Bukhari*, vol 6, no 510, pp 478-80.
7. *Sahih Al-Bukhari*, vol. 5, p. 96.
8. Ibn Abi Dawud, *Kitab al Masahif*, p.15
9. Crawford, Craig. *The Prophecies: A Journey to the End of Time*, p. 19-20.
10. Harman, H.M., *Introduction to the Study of the Holy Scriptures*, p.488.
11. Ibid, p. 465.
12. Ibid, p. 464-465
13. Ibid, p.463-464
14. Barrows, M., *The Dead Sea Scrolls*, p. 73-101.
15. Broyles, C.C., *The Redeeming King: Psalm 72's Contribution to the Messianic Ideal*, pp. 23-25.
16. Harman, p. 52
17. Kassis, *A Concordance of the Qur'an*, p. 483
18. Pickthall, *The Meaning of the Glorious Qur'an*, p. 47
19. Abdullah Yusuf Ali, *The Meaning of the Holy Qur'an*, Note 53
20. Kassis, *A Concordance of the Qur'an*, page 595
21. The *Hadith* is known as the Muslim *Traditions* and is a narration of what Muhammad said or did. It is considered an expression of divine revelation. It is accepted as a chief source of Islamic belief and practice and is second in authority only to the Qur'an.
22. *Sahih AL-Bukhari*, 9:357 (see also AL-Bukhari, part 8, Bab TahaagAdam wa Musa.)
23. Smith, Chuck, *Answers for Today*, p. 128
24. Karim, *Mishkatul Masabih*, vol. 3, p.760
25. *Sahih AL-Bukhari*, 9:423
26. Ibid, 4:552
27. Ibid, 8:238
28. Ibid, 4:501
29. AL-Tabari, *Ta'rikh ar-rusul wa'l - mu luk*, Volume 1, pp 135-

139

30. Shorter, *Encyclopedia of Islam*, p. 175
31. Abdullah Yusuf Ali, *The Holy Qur'an*, page 1149. Note 4096
32. NOTE: The Arabic word "Injeel" also means "Good News." Another word for gospel is "evangel" which is a word derived from the Greek word "evangelion." The Arabic equivalent is Injeel. Therefore, "Injeel" or the "Good News" is the Holy Book about Al-Masih Isa.
33. AL-Baidawi commenting on Q. Surah 2:253
34. Yousef al-Qaradawi and others, *t-Twahid*, p. 98
35. Sabbaki, *At-tabaqat al*; Shafe' eiah al-Kubr, Volume 6. p. 235
36. Harry Austryn Walfson, *The Philosophy of the Kalam*, Harvard University Press, 1976, p. 251; quoted from Fisal Volume II, p.5-6; and Volume III, p. 5.
37. Ibid, p. 240-241 quoted from AL-Tabari, Annals, P. 118, Volume II. 10-11
38. *Al-Ahadith Al-Qudsiyyah*, Divine Narratives, Hadith 112, page 156-157
39. AL-Baidawi, commenting on Q. Surah 4:171
40. Abdullah Yusuf Ali, Note 5365
41. *Sahih AL-Bukhari*, anbiya, commentary on Surah 17 (al-Isra); Muslim, iman 46; At-Tirmidhi, qiyama 10; al-Musnad, volume 2, p. 436; volume 5, pp. 292, 314.
42. The word "ransom" means to "buy back." It is the payment demanded for the freedom of a captive.
43. "Redeem" is defined in the dictionary as: to free or rescue by paying a price or to free from the consequences of sin.
44. Halverson, D.C., *The Compact Guide to World Religions*
45. *Mishkat*, Book IV, chapter 49
46. *Mishkat*, Book IV, chapter 42, section 2
47. *Sahih AL-Bukhari*, 4:501 and 8:238.
48. Part 4, page 237
49. "Legal Opinion" part 6, page 41
50. Refer to *The Successors of the Apostle*, bu Khalid Muhammad Khalid, page 114
51. AL Jalalan, p. 451
52. Assfy, *Islam and Christianity*, p.6
53. Halverson, Ibid.
54. Kateregga and Shenk, *Islam and Christianity*, p. 19
55. Ibid, p. 97, 98
56. John Gilchrist, *The Christian Witness to Muslims*, p. 337.
57. *Sahih AL-Bukhari*, 6:71
58. Nurbakhash, Javad, *Jesus in the Eyes of the Sufis*, p. 53-54

59. *Sahih AL-Bukhari*, Arabic-English, Dar al Fikr, 4:506
60. AL-Baidawi commenting on Q. Surah 3:36
61. *Sahih AL-Bukhari* 6:71
62. *vide Mishkat*, Bab 25, Fasl 1:1, Bab and Fasl 3:1
63. Suyuti Commenting on Q, Surah 3:36.
64. *Sahih AL-Bukhari*, 4:501
65. *Sahih AL-Bukhari*, Arabic-English, Dar al-Fikr, 8:319
66. Ibid, 8:408 and 8:379
67. Ibid, 5:715: "O Allah! Forgive me, and bestow your mercy on me,..."
68. Ibid, 6:236
69. *Towards an Islamic Christology II*, The Muslim World, Vol. LXX, No. 2, April 1980, P. 93
70. AL-Baidawi commenting on Q. Surah 5:110
71. Please read Injeel, Mark 2:1-12
72. AL-Baidawi commenting on Q. Surah 5:110
73. Baidawi, commenting on Surah 5:110
74. AL-Baidawi commenting on Q. Surah 3:45
75. Parrinder, G. *Jesus in the Qur'an*, p. 121
76. Abdullah Yusuf Ali, Footnote 2469
77. Obaray, *Miraculous Conception, Death, Resurrection and Ascension of Jesus as taught in the Qur'an*, p. 45
78. The Azhar University in Egypt has been regarded as the light of Islam for the entire Islamic world.
79. Dr. Mahmud Shaltut, *Quoted in the Muslim World*, xxxiv, pp. 214f
80. Abdullah Yusuf Ali, Footnote 663
81. Ibid, Footnote 664
82. Maududi, *The Meaning of the Qur'an*, p.390
83. Daryabadi, *The Holy Qur'an*, Volume 1, page 96-A
84. Payne, J. Barton, *Encyclopedia of Biblical Prophecy*, p. 317
85. DAR AL HALAL
86. Flavius Josephus, *The Complete Works of Josephus*, p. VI-IX, *Antiquities of the Jews,* Book XVIII, Chapter III, Section 3
87. Ibid, p. 379.
88. AL-Razi, *Al-Tafsir Al-Kabir* commenting on Q. Surah 4:158
89. Ibid, commenting on Q. Surah 3:55
90. Ibid, commenting on Q. Surah 4:158
91. Abdullah Yusuf Ali, Footnote 4662
92. Alam, Nuzul-e-Esa: *Descencion of Jesus Christ*, p. 37
93. *Sahih AL-Bukhari*, 4:437
94. Ibid, 3:425 and 4:657
95. *Sahih Muslim*, English Translation, Hadith No. 7037

96. *Sahih Al-Bukhari*, English-Arabic, 2:459
97. Ibid, 9:243 and 2:459
98. Suyuti commenting on Q. Surah 6:158
99. *Sahih Muslim*, English Translation, Kitab AL Fitan Wa Ashrat As-sa'ah, Hadith No. 2897
100. *Sahih Muslim*, Volume 1, p. 93
101. *Sahih Muslim*, Kitab AL-Fitan wa Ashrat-As-Sa'ah (English translation), Hadith No. 7015
102. Ibid; Hadith No. 7000
103. He said, "in the name" not "in the names" (singular not plural).
104. Al-Qartaby commenting on Q. Surah 4:171
105. Smith, John Pye, *The Scripture Testimony to the Messiah*, Volume II, p.454
106. Halverson, Ibid
107. AL-Ghazzali, *Ihya' Ulumed-Din*, 4:263
108. Shaarani, *Book of Yamakeet*, p. 11
109. Arberry, A.J., *Revelation and Reason in Islam*, p. 22
110. Imam Abi Hanifah, *Al-Fiqh al-Akbar*, p.33
111. Parrinder, G., *Jesus in the Qur'an*.
112. Schaff, Philip, *The Creeds of Christendom: with a History and Critical Notes*.
113. Cragg, A. Kenneth, *The Call of the Minaret*, p. 290
114. Abdullah Yusuf Ali, Footnote 4679
115. A. Guillaume, *Life of Muhammad*, A Translation of Ibn Ishaq's SIRAT ARASUL, p. 657
116. Al-Razi, commenting on Surah 3:39
117. Ibid
118. *Sahih AL-Bukhari* 6:229
119. Tabary commenting on Surah 3:39
120. Ibn Kathir commenting on Q. Surah 3:39
121. AL-Razi commenting on Q. Surah 3:39; and Suyuti commenting on Q. Surah 3:39
122. AL-Razi, *Al-Tafsir Al-Kabir*, commenting on Q. Surah 19:7
123. Baydawi (p. 457), AL Jalalan (p. 288) and in the Kash-shaf of the Al Zamkhashri (part 3, p. 192),
124. *AL-Maqsad AL-Asna*, p. 91
125. Stade, *Ninety-Nine Names of God in Islam*, p. 91